BACKROADS
OF THE GREAT
American
WEST

BACKROADS OF THE GREAT American WEST

YOUR GUIDE TO GREAT DAY TRIPS AND WEEKEND GETAWAYS

GARY CRABBE

DIANA FAIRBANKS

JIM HINCKLEY

THERESA HUSARIK

KAREN MISURACA

GEORGE OSTERTAG

RHONDA OSTERTAG

MIKE SEDAM

CLAUDE WIATROWSKI

DAVID M. WYMAN

motorbooks

Contents

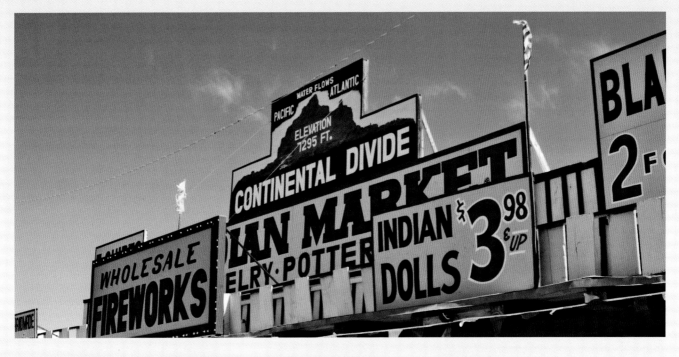

Chapter 1

COLORADO

THE MILLION DOLLAR

HIGHWAY NEAR OURAY,

COLORADO. DAWN WILSON

PHOTO/SHUTTERSTOCK

By Claude Wiatrowski

STONE, COAL, and SILVER

MARBLE TO ASPEN

CRYSTAL MILL NEAR MARBLE IS ONE OF THE
MOST PHOTOGRAPHED SITES IN COLORADO.
PETER KUNASZ/SHUTTERSTOCK

COLORADO HIGHWAY 133 AND COUNTY ROAD 3 PROVIDE ACCESS TO THE CRYSTAL RIVER VALLEY, A REMARKABLE PLACE. THE INDUSTRIES OF COAL MINING AND MARBLE QUARRYING AND FINISHING DOMINATED THE AREA IN THE LATE NINETEENTH AND EARLY TWENTIETH CENTURIES. TRAINS OF SIX DIFFERENT RAILROADS CHUGGED OR WHIRRED (ONE WAS ELECTRIC) IN THE 40-MILE-LONG (64.4. KM) VALLEY. THIS PLACE IS EVER SO REMARKABLE BECAUSE THERE IS MUCH TO EXPLORE ALONG THE CRYSTAL RIVER NEAR A HEAVILY DEVELOPED AREA OF COLORADO THAT HAS LOST MUCH OF ITS HISTORIC AMBIANCE. YOUR JOURNEY STARTS IN THE TOWN OF MARBLE.

By 1907, blocks of marble were being quarried southwest of the town of Marble, and teamsters gingerly dropped them down the mountainside in wagons. Workmen were constructing the marble-finishing mill, some of it built from marble! An electric railway, the Yule Tram, began hauling marble from the Yule Quarry in 1910, down a surrealistically steep electric railroad. Eventually, two railroads would haul the huge marble blocks from quarries to the finishing mill. The brilliant white stone was shipped to the rest of the country on trains of the Crystal River & San Juan Railway. Marble for the Lincoln Memorial was wrested from the earth at the Yule Quarry and cut and polished in the mill at Marble. In 1931, the marble block for the Tomb of the Unknown Soldier was quarried here. So heavy was this single block that it was carefully lowered from the quarry to the mill at 1 mile (1.6 km) per day. Closed in 1917, the mill was rehabilitated and reopened in 1922. The mill and quarry railroad were dismantled in 1941. Trucks now carry marble down the old steep railroad grade from the quarry.

The ruins of the Colorado-Yule Marble Company mill are fascinating and extend for about half a mile (0.8 km) along the river bank. An operator once stood by the now-rusting conveyor that pokes its head out of a marble-walled building. You can imagine the long-gone overhead crane struggling with huge blocks of white stone as it rolled along on rails supported by the large, marble pillars that still dot the mill site. Farther north, explore the marble graveyard where partially processed but defective pieces of marble were discarded. This area is protected, so please do not remove souvenirs. You can see marble debris alongside the Crystal River where it was dumped to stabilize the river bank. Near the mill parking area in Marble is the turntable pit that spun locomotives of the Crystal River & San Juan end for end to begin their return journey to Carbondale. That pit was once lined with marble blocks! A Marble Historical Society museum will help you orient yourself to this formerly bustling industrial complex and the town that supported it. Drive north on County Road 3 for 6 miles (9.7 km) and turn right on Colorado Highway 133.

About 5 miles (8 km) downstream, the white of marble turns to the black of coal at Redstone. A railroad brought coal down from the Coal Basin mines to be processed into coke by the huge Redstone industrial complex. Coke is mostly carbon, the energy-carrying component of coal. The coke was shipped to the Colorado Fuel & Iron steel mill at Pueblo. Redstone was a company town, with the mining

company providing the store, library, town band, and other amenities. Liquor was always a problem in mining towns. Outlawing alcohol never worked, because miners simply traveled to the nearest source of the forbidden beverage. John Osgood, the man who developed the Redstone coal complex and fathered the Pueblo steel mill, had a unique solution. The miners' clubs at both Redstone and Coal Basin offered liquor but would not allow one man to buy another a drink. Without the cry of "this round is on me," the endless parade of men reciprocating the favor was avoided.

A severe depression, known as the Silver Panic, shut down the Crystal River Railroad to Redstone in 1893, the very year it was constructed. Trains sat idle until 1899. Coal production ended so suddenly in 1909 that residents had to leave many of their belongings to catch the last train out of Redstone for Carbondale. Osgood attempted to

reopen the town's industrial complex many times but without success.

None of Redstone's sizeable industrial plant remains, with the exception of some beehive coke ovens hear the highway. Drive into town to see the Redstone Inn, now a hotel but originally built in 1901 as housing for single workmen. Osgood built a home here in 1903, a not-so-modest castle named Cleveholm Manor, for a mere $500,000. His castle still stands, though its fortunes have been constantly changing. Check to see if tours or lodging might be available. If not, you can glimpse the castle south of town across the river through the trees. Continue north on Colorado 133.

Carbondale sits at the north end of the Crystal River where its waters empty into the Roaring Fork River. Carbondale's roots are agricultural, though its history was strongly influenced by Aspen's silver mines, Redstone's coal mines, and Marble's

Your Recreation Fees At Work

NOTICE

ENJOY
BUT DO NOT DESTROY
YOUR AMERICAN HERITAGE

NO DOGS ALLOWED
IN THE GHOST TOWN
OF ASHCROFT

quarries. The first settlers arrived in the 1880s and Carbondale was incorporated in 1888. Three railroads—the Crystal River, the Colorado Midland, and the Denver & Rio Grande—once served the town, but none remain. Agriculture has declined in importance, as Carbondale is flanked by two huge tourist destinations: Aspen and Glenwood Springs. Learn about Carbondale's agricultural and coal-mining past at the Thompson House Museum. At the north end of Carbondale turn right from Colorado 133 onto Colorado Highway 82 bound for Aspen.

Basalt was a junction on the spaghetti-like complexity of Colorado's railroad network. Denver & Rio Grande trains from Glenwood Springs whistled through Basalt on their way to Aspen. The Colorado Midland's death-defying crossing of the continental divide at

Hagerman Tunnel brought its trains to Basalt, where some trains continued west to Grand Junction and others branched south to Aspen.

Colorado 82 bypasses downtown Basalt. To drive through downtown, make a left turn onto the first exit for Two Rivers Road. If you'd rather not drive unpaved mountain roads, continue eastbound on Two Rivers Road until it joins with Colorado 82 again toward Aspen and skip to the section titled Ashcroft. Otherwise continue your journey to Ruedi Reservoir and Ivanhoe Lake.

From Two Rivers Road, make a left turn (northeast) onto Midland Ave. which becomes Frying Pan Road. Drive east on Frying Pan Road (County Road 4, Forest Road 105) which mostly follows the Colorado Midland Railway grade. You'll pass Ruedi Reservoir,

IN 1953, THE ASHCROFT TOWN SITE WAS DEEDED TO THE FOREST SERVICE. IN 1974, THE ASPEN HISTORICAL SOCIETY BEGAN A PROJECT TO RESTORE AND PRESERVE ITS REMAINING BUILDINGS.
KRISTI BLOKHIN/SHUTTERSTOCK

A VIEW EAST ALONG COOPER AVE. IN DOWNTOWN ASPEN. THE SKI AREA IS VISIBLE IN THE BACKGROUND. *OSCITY/SHUTTERSTOCK*

drive by the charcoal ovens at Sellar and traverse the rocky shelf upon which trains perched at Hell Gate where you can look down and see pieces of a wrecked locomotive tender. About 1.7 miles (2.7 km) past Hell Gate, the road diverges. You must take the Ivanhoe Lake Road (Forest 527) to the right and finally enjoy the alpine beauty of Lake Ivanhoe. East of the lake, you can easily spot the lower railroad tunnel, the Busk-Ivanhoe Railroad Tunnel. It is now named the Carlton Tunnel and transports water from Colorado's western slope to its eastern slope. The higher Hagerman Railroad Tunnel is a little more difficult to find so ask locally

or have good maps on hand. Return to Basalt on the same route. Turn left (east) on Two Rivers Road to return to Colorado 82 but this time east of Basalt. Turn left onto Colorado 82 for Aspen.

Just before reaching Aspen, you'll encounter a roundabout. Use it to take the Castle Creek Road south and watch for the ghost town of Ashcroft.

In 1880, men scurried about to locate five hundred optimistic lots at the town site of Ashcroft. By 1881, children skipped along Ashcroft's streets to a public school. Adults waited anxiously for daily mail. Important messages were swiftly conveyed on the electric telegraph wire. By 1885,

its population peaked at 2,500, though many left during the harsh winters. Along Ashcroft's lively streets, miners stumbled out of seventeen saloons, traveling salesmen struggled with sample cases at eight hotels, and families went bowling. But the sound of the train whistle echoing up the valley from Aspen, just downstream along Castle Creek, was the beginning of the end for Ashcroft, and today it is a ghost town.

In 1953, the town was deeded to the Forest Service and, in 1974, the Aspen Historical Society began a project to restore and preserve its remaining buildings. There are few Colorado ghost

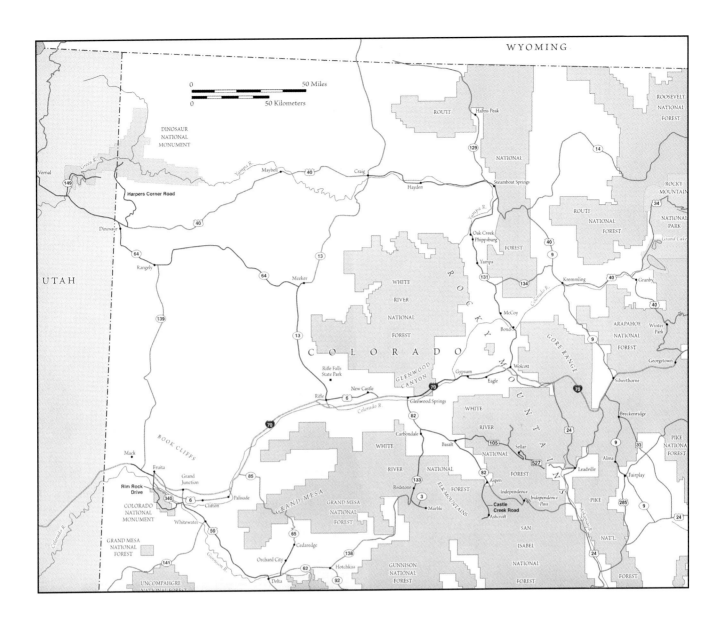

towns with Ashcroft's large stand of old buildings. More importantly, Ashcroft is Colorado's most easily accessed ghost town of its size. It is just 10 miles (16.1 km) south of Aspen along a paved road and is handicap accessible. If you want to experience an authentic Colorado ghost town without an adventurous road trip, Ashcroft is your destination. Retrace your steps back to the roundabout to continue into Aspen.

In 1879, prospectors discovered silver in the Roaring Fork Valley, nestled between the Sawatch Range and Elk Mountains, and Aspen was incorporated just a year later. Mines bustled with activity and a smelter gushed noxious fumes into the sky, creating wealth in the process. All that was missing for prosperity was reliable and efficient transportation. Two railroads, the Colorado Midland and the Denver & Rio Grande, arrived in 1887 and Aspen boomed. It was Colorado's third largest city by 1892 with over 12,000 residents. Trolleys, churches, saloons, prostitution, gambling—Aspen had everything a wealthy mining town needed! The repeal of the Sherman Silver Purchase Act in 1893, however, devastated Aspen as it did all Colorado's silvered cities.

Aspen's miners hiked up the slopes above town to reach work and slid down on "boards" to return home. The region's first ski resort, at Ashcroft, appeared in the 1930s but it was not until after World War II that Aspen's famous ski industry blossomed. After the war, summer cultural activities began to grow in Aspen with the support of Chicago industrialist Walter Paepcke. Music festivals, scientific institutes, and instructional programs continue to fill the summer months.

Aspen's downtown is home to many restored historic structures including the Wheeler Opera House and the Hotel Jerome. The Wheeler/Stallard Museum chronicles Aspen's history and is one of several facilities operated by the Aspen Historical Society.

By Claude Wiatrowski

San Juan
SKYWAY

DURANGO TO MANCOS

THE DURANGO & SILVERTON NARROW GAUGE
RAILROAD'S RESTORED STEAM LOCOMOTIVE RUNS
AS A VISITOR ATTRACTION OUT OF DURANGO.

FLORIDA STOCK/SHUTTERSTOCK

AFTER TRESPASSING ON UTE LANDS TO EXPLORE THE SAN JUAN MOUNTAINS, WHITE PROSPECTORS AGITATED FOR THE UTES TO BE REMOVED. THE 1873 BRUNOT TREATY SOLD FOUR MILLION ACRES OF UTE LAND IN THE SAN JUANS, AND MUCH MORE WOULD EVENTUALLY BE TAKEN IN THE SEARCH FOR RICHES. DEVELOPMENT OF SOUTHWESTERN COLORADO BOOMED AFTER THAT TREATY WAS SIGNED. THIS IS THE LONGEST AND MOST COMPLEX COLORADO JOURNEY DESCRIBED HERE, SO IT WOULD BE PRUDENT TO START VERY EARLY IN THE MORNING ESPECIALLY IF YOU WISH TO EXPLORE ALL THE SIDE TRIPS. ALTERNATELY, YOU MIGHT DECIDE TO SPLIT THIS JOURNEY INTO TWO DAYS INSTEAD OF ONE. START TODAY'S JOURNEY IN THE BUSTLING TOWN OF DURANGO.

The Denver & Rio Grande Railroad founded the city of Durango in 1880 as a home for its roundhouse and other facilities. Ignoring the existing hamlet of Hermosa, the railroad made more money creating Durango and reaped the profits from increased land values due to the railroad's very presence. Though the Denver & Rio Grande no longer serves Durango, the narrow-gauge trains to Silverton are now operated by the Durango & Silverton Narrow Gauge Railroad. The train boards from the original depot, and half the roundhouse is now a superb museum. Downtown offers both original historic buildings, including the 1887 Strater Hotel, as well as new buildings constructed in the style of the old. Though not in downtown, you can tour the Animas Museum.

Durango's Fort Lewis College began as an Indian school, established in 1891 after the Army's fort was deactivated. It was 16 miles (25.7 km) southwest of Durango on the Ute Mountain Reservation and moved to its present

THE GHOST TOWN OF ANIMAS FORKS, AT AN ALTITUDE OF 11,200 FEET, FEATURES A NUMBER OF STANDING BUILDINGS, THE OLDEST OF WHICH WAS BUILT IN 1873. A WALKING-TOUR BROCHURE IS HIGHLY RECOMMENDED. *KRIS WIKTOR/ SHUTTERSTOCK*

location on a mesa overlooking Durango in 1956. Drive north on US 550 to Silverton

Silverton was connected to Durango by railroad in 1882. Its population peaked at around five thousand souls. Those nineteenth-century mountain pioneers dined at restaurants that served fine wines with lobster in the remote San Juan Mountains. The wealth that gave birth to elegance in this small mountain valley was tapped by four railroads that moved ore to and from three smelters and thirty mills. Silverton has also seen rough times. The Silver Panic arrived in 1893; the 1918 flu epidemic decimated the already-dwindling population; metal prices fell; a mountain lake collapsed into a mine; and the last major mine closed in 1991. After World War II, however, both Hollywood and tourists discovered Silverton. Movies were filmed here and, as quite a surprise to the railroad, the Denver & Rio Grande's narrow-gauge, steam-powered trains from Durango began to carry passengers again—lots of passengers.

That railroad, now the Durango & Silverton Narrow Gauge Railroad, operates the Freight Yard Museum in the old Silverton depot. Here, you'll see a model of the Silverton Railway's Corkscrew Turntable and learn about its heart-stopping operations. You can see,

or even stay at, the Grand Imperial Hotel built in 1883, and visit the San Juan County Historical Society Museum. If you are not adventurous or have run out of time, continue north on US 550 and skip to the section titled Million Dollar Highway

If you crave adventure and are willing to drive on unpaved roads, follow the Animas River northeast out of Silverton on County Road 2. This optional portion of your journey might require three or four hours or more. The grade of the abandoned Silverton Northern Railroad also follows the river. Stop at the overlook and interpretive exhibit at the site of the Silver Lake Mill. The

Waldheim mansion once stood on the riverbank below you, as did the huge Silver Lake Mill. In the distance, you'll see the Mayflower Mill, which will be your next stop.

The Mayflower was the last mill to close in the district—it ceased operations along with the Sunnyside Mine in 1991. Unlike most historic mills, the Mayflower was left intact. It was built in the 1930s when its machinery was moved into place via the now-gone Silverton Northern Railroad. With the railroad gone and old machinery not in demand, it was best to donate the intact industrial plant to the San Juan County Historical Society. The

Mayflower is the most complete historic mill left in Colorado. A self-guided tour will let you explore as many or as few details as you wish . . . and there is much to explore. Don't miss the cable tramway that carries ore buckets (still hanging on the cable) from the mine high on the mountainside across from the mill. Bring your binoculars or a long telephoto lens on your camera to glimpse the tramway's distant eastern terminus.

Continue north until you reach the town site of Eureka. Little is left of the mill at Eureka, but its foundations are clearly visible on the mountainside. Your road crosses over to the south side of the river and becomes the old railroad grade. The next and last 4 miles (6.4 km) of the railroad were also the first to be abandoned. Railroad builder Otto Mears had offered to extend his railroad to Animas Forks, so the mines, mills, and railroad could operate year-round, but the first winter saw the railroad closed by hundreds of inches of snow. Mears prepared for the next winter by

enclosing most of those 4 miles (6.4 km) of track in timber snow sheds. Imagine the sinking feeling—shared by Mears, the mine owners, and the 450 Animas Forks residents—when the first avalanche of the season wiped out Mears's investment in those structures! Drive those last 4 miles to 11,200 foot-high (3,414 m) Animas Forks, where a surprising number of buildings stand, the oldest of which was built in 1873. A highly recommended walking tour brochure for this ghost town will help orient you. Before the railroad arrived in 1904, the town was supplied from Lake City via the Cinnamon Pass Road, today a road suitable only for four-wheel drive vehicles. Return to Silverton and continue north on US 550.

Otto Mears built a toll road between Ouray and Ironton in 1883. It would eventually reach Silverton and be called the Million Dollar Highway for, supposedly, the modern highway cost millions of dollars per mile to construct between Ouray and the summit of Red Mountain Pass. Another story is that the

fill material used to build the highway was actually ore containing millions of dollars of gold. The truth is lost, along with the other barroom conversations of 1920's Silverton.

Climbing the Million Dollar Highway, you'll pass the surface plant of the Idarado Mine on your right. Near the mine, turn left into a well-marked overlook with an exceptional view of, and great interpretive signs about, the Red Mountain Mining District. You'll be stunned at the panoramic scope of the district and the seemingly impossible route of the Silverton Railway. Think about how much wealth must have created this huge industrial area, much of which is over eleven thousand feet high and covered in feet of winter snow. Remember that this is just one of several mining districts in the area!

Driving today's circuitous paved highways, it is difficult to understand that Telluride, Ouray, Silverton, and Lake City were all really part of the same mineral-rich locale. You have to escape to steep, rocky tracks—the province of

four-wheel-drive vehicles and mountain goats—to see how close these towns are to each other. Continue north on US 550 to Ouray.

Ouray was incorporated in 1876, the hundredth year of the existence of the United States. Prospectors arrived here a year earlier. In 1887, the Denver & Rio Grande built a narrow-gauge track from Montrose to Ouray, but steep rocky walls made railroad construction impossible in every other compass direction. Ironton's ore, which had been hauled down a difficult toll road to Ouray, now found the route to Silverton an easy trip on the new Silverton Railway, which was completed in 1889.

Ouray never experienced a devastating fire, so many of its nineteenth-century buildings still stand. A walk around town is a must. St. Joseph's Miners' Hospital opened its doors in 1887, and its building now hosts the Ouray County Museum. Continue north on US Highway 550 to Ridgway.

The Ridgway Railroad Museum is located at the junction of US 550 and Colorado Highway 62. The Rio Grande Southern Railroad's shops were located in Ridgway, incorporated in 1891. That same year, tourists had started traveling by train to the summit of Pikes Peak as luxury hotels and fine restaurants catered to wealthy visitors up and down Colorado's eastern mountains. In contrast, southwestern Colorado was still remote and rugged. Otto Mears's construction of the Rio Grande Southern Railroad was about to open up this isolated land. Mears had built the Silverton Railroad, but it fell short of reaching Ouray by a rugged 8 miles (12.9 km). To bridge this tiny gap, he built 162 miles of the Rio Grande Southern! A train journey from Silverton to Ouray started on the Denver & Rio Grande branch line from Silverton to Durango, continued over Lizard Head Pass and ended on another Denver & Rio Grande branch line from Ridgway to Ouray. You can only wonder how

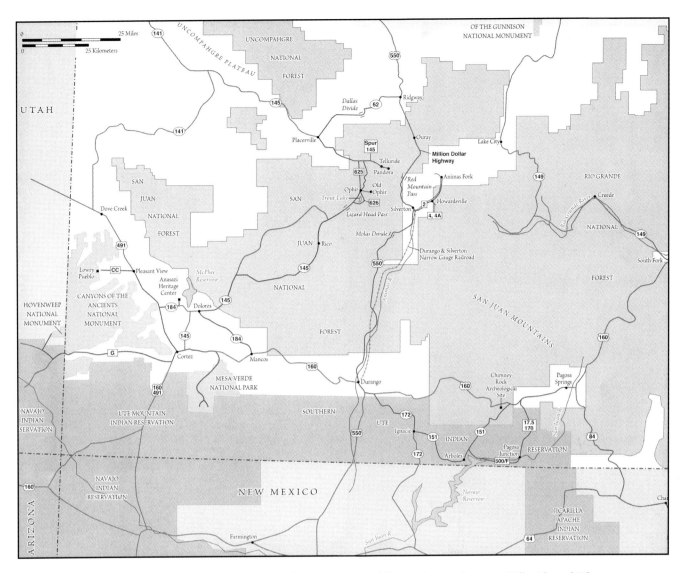

many people chose this 235-mile train trip instead of the 8-mile bone-breaking jaunt in a stagecoach.

The Rio Grande Southern served mines, logging stands, ranches, and small towns. But it never generated much traffic. All its almost fifty locomotives were purchased second hand. It couldn't even pay its operating expenses, let alone return the investors' capital used to build this spectacular railroad. It survived only sixty years, a short lifespan for a railroad.

On most of the remainder of this journey, you will be following the route of the Rio Grande Southern Railway. After visiting the Ridgway Railroad Museum, drive west on Colorado Highway 62. At Placerville, go left on Colorado Highway 145.

You will arrive at a roundabout. Use it to continue on Colorado Spur 145 to Telluride, a showplace mining town with the same nineteenth-century amenities as Aspen, Cripple Creek, or Leadville. Founded in 1878 as Columbia, its name was changed to Telluride in 1887. Gold was first discovered here in 1858 but development was slow because of its remote location until the 1890 arrival of the Rio Grande Southern Railroad. Infamous Butch Cassidy's first major crime was robbing Telluride's San Miguel Valley Bank in 1889. All of Telluride's historic mines—including the Pandora, Sheridan, Smuggler-Union, and Tomboy—were eventually consolidated into the Idarado Mining Company. Its extensive network of tunnels undermines the entire area

between Telluride and Silverton.

During World War II, worthless uranium ore that had been accumulating in the waste dumps of mines was hauled away by narrow-gauge steam trains for refinement into fuel for the world's first atomic weapons. Armed federal agents rode the antique steam trains from Telluride.

The first ski lift was installed in Telluride in 1972 and skiing slowly replaced mining as Telluride's major industry. As the final ore was being trundled out of the Pandora Mine, tourism became a year-round business with summer activities augmenting skiing. There are still many historic structures in Telluride including the legendary New Sheridan Hotel. The Telluride Historical Museum is

CONTINUE THROUGH DOLORES ON COLORADO 145
AND THEN MAKE A RIGHT TURN ONTO COLORADO
HIGHWAY 184 WESTBOUND TO THE CANYON OF THE
ANCIENTS VISITOR CENTER, A MUSEUM OF ANCIENT
PUEBLOAN AND OTHER NATIVE CULTURES.
MARAP/SHUTTERSTOCK

housed in the historic Miner's Hospital building. Return on Colorado Spur 145 to the roundabout and use it to follow Colorado 145 south.

The mining town of Ophir, named after the biblical location of King Solomon's mines, was the western end of the Ophir Loop, a special section of railroad track. Trains dropped down the mountainside from Trout Lake, circled back at Ophir, and rolled down the valley of the South Fork of the San Miguel River just below the upper track. If you wish to avoid dirt road travel, continue on Colorado 145 and skip ahead to Lizard Head Pass.

At Ophir, turn right on County Road 63L (Forest Road 625) down the San Miguel River Valley. In about 1 mile, a very sharp left turn onto Ames Road leads to the Ames power plant. Ames was the location of the world's first commercial alternating-current power plant. By the spring of 1891, the plant was supplying current to run the pumps that drained the Gold King Mine, 3.5 miles distant. Thomas Edison championed direct current which could not be sent long distances. Nikola Tesla and the Westinghouse Electric Company promoted alternating current which, though unproven, was claimed to be able to reach the mine. The mine's owners had no choice but to gamble on alternating current. The mines were flooding and no other source of energy was a viable option. This hydroelectric plant's turbines were spun by water from Trout Lake. A newer plant replaced the original and still operates today here at the same location.

Back on Forest Road 625, you'll pass a stone building at Ilium, another power plant which reused the water from the Ames plant to generate more electricity. Farther along and west across the river, you can see a large timber structure used to store and load coal into steam locomotive tenders. You are also near Vance Junction where a branch line track diverged to serve Telluride. This road continues to Colorado 145 and the Telluride roundabout, but I would advise that, after you see the railroad coaling structure, you simply turn around and drive to Colorado 145 at Ophir.

About 3 miles south of Ophir, turn left onto County Road 63A (North Trout Lake Road, Forest Road 626.) A railroad water tank will appear on your left. Farther ahead there is a timber railroad trestle on your right bridging a small stream that runs into Trout Lake. Continue on this road back to Colorado 145 at the summit of Lizard Head Pass. Turn left (south) onto the highway.

The Rio Grande Southern crested 10,222-foot Lizard Head Pass where today you can examine a display about the railroad's history. It maintained a wye here (a track for turning locomotives and snowplows) as well as stock pens. Every fall, huge trains of sheep—some requiring four locomotives—were loaded here and at other stations onto double-decked narrow-gauge stock cars for a trip to lower winter ranges or for a final trip to the stockyards. These stock rushes occurred all over Colorado but were especially spectacular on the Rio Grande Southern, a railroad that slumbered most of the year with very few trains. The last stock rush on the Rio Grande Southern occurred in 1949 when a half million sheep were moved by just this one railroad. Its trains hauled thousands of cars full of the wooly creatures behind every antique steam locomotive that could be made to move!

Rico is the Spanish word for "rich." Gold was found at the town of Rico during the Civil War. The discovery of a rich lode of silver in 1879 literally put the town on the map. The Rio Grande Southern's trains reached Rico in 1891. In 1892, the railroad built a mountainous branch to the mines east of town. Rico's population reached five thousand and the usual mining town diversions—twenty-three saloons and a red-light district—took root. Nevertheless, a bank, churches, a theater, a boarding house, and the railroad seemed to assure future prosperity. Then came repeal of the Sherman Silver Purchase Act in 1893. The town's economy vanished almost overnight. Trains no longer rumbled from the mines with loads of silver, and the track to the mines was removed. By 1900, only eight hundred stubborn souls clung to a rugged existence in Rico. Mining recovered in the 1920s and eventually shifted its focus from silver to lead and zinc.

Downtown Rico displays many historic structures including a wonderful stone courthouse. The railroad yard was west of the highway and its most significant remnant is the water tank that filled the tenders of thirsty steam locomotives about to climb Lizard Head Pass. You can't miss the surface plants of some of the historic mines that are just north of town.

Dolores was incorporated in 1900 and served the lumber industry. A tangle of logging railroads spread north from town. To convert those logs into lumber, a sawmill was built at the new town of McPhee, now submerged under the waters of the McPhee reservoir.

Dolores is home to Galloping Goose No. 5. A Galloping Goose is a gasoline-powered railcar—originally built from old automobiles and later from old buses. Just a single employee would welcome the few passengers aboard, load the mail and possibly some small parcels of freight, and then drive the Goose down the rails—a perfect solution for a remote railroad with little traffic. Goose No. 5 usually rests on rails outside a reconstruction of the Dolores railroad depot, which houses both the Rio Grande Southern Railroad Museum and the Dolores Visitors' Center. This small but excellent museum chronicles the history of the railroad and its flock of Geese. Goose No. 5 occasionally flies away, trucked to the narrow-gauge railroads at Durango or Chama, New Mexico to again gallop down the rails.

Continue through Dolores on Colorado 145 and then make a right turn onto Colorado Highway 184 westbound. The Canyon of the Ancients Visitor Center and Museum, on your right, is a museum of Ancient Puebloan and other native cultures. The Center is the perfect introduction to Ancient Puebloan culture, and there are two ruins on site. It is also the gateway to Canyons of the Ancients National Monument: 164,000 acres containing about six thousand ruins, mostly unexcavated and undeveloped. Continue west on Colorado 184 and make a left turn on US Highway 491 to reach Cortez.

Though not part of this journey, Mesa Verde National Park is near Cortez if you wish to extend your stay and view its spectacular array of cliff dwellings. The entrance to Mesa Verde National Park is 10 miles east of Cortez on US Highway 160. You should allow most of a day to see the National Park.

By Claude Wiatrowski

DONKEYS ARE PULLED UP A CRIPPLE CREEK
STREET IN PREPARATION FOR RACES. CRIPPLE
CREEK'S HISTORIC DOWNTOWN IS FILLED WITH
NEW GAMBLING CASINOS BEHIND THE HISTORIC
FACADES OF ORIGINAL BUILDINGS.
VICKI L. MILLER/SHUTTERSTOCK

CRIPPLE CREEK Gold

CASCADE TO WESTCLIFFE

UTE INDIANS TRAVELED WEST OVER THE PASS THAT NOW BEARS THE TRIBE'S NAME. LATER, EUROPEAN EXPLORERS ALSO TRUDGED UP UTE PASS FROM THE CITY OF MANITOU SPRINGS. COMMERCE WITH THE SOUTH PARK MINING TOWNS WAS CONDUCTED BY HORSE-DRAWN WAGON BEFORE THE TRAINS OF THE COLORADO MIDLAND RAILWAY CHUGGED INTO THE MOUNTAINS VIA THIS SAME PASSAGE THROUGH THE MOUNTAINS. BEGIN YOUR JOURNEY BY DRIVING WEST FROM MANITOU SPRINGS ON US HIGHWAY 24 TOWARD DIVIDE.

The Cascade town company was formed in 1886 shortly after plans for the railroad were announced. Construction of the elegant Ramona Hotel began in 1888 as Cascade and other Ute Pass towns became high-elevation escapes from the summer heat. That same year, the Pikes Peak toll road was completed from Cascade to the summit of "America's mountain." Permanent summer residences appeared including Marigreen Pines, the mansion of Thomas Cusack. Now a religious community, the mansion will be above the stone wall on your right as you drive into Cascade. The Ramona Hotel is no more but many other historic buildings, especially older residences, still enjoy the coolness of summer.

In 1890, the Ute Pass Land and Water Company began development of a summer resort community, which would become Chipita Park. Cottages surrounded the Ute Hotel, which hovered over a red sandstone railroad depot and a man-made lake. Little development occurred until Frank Marcroft gained control of the company in 1927, named the community Chipita Park (after Chipeta, the wife of Ute chief Ouray), and aggressively promoted land sales.

In contrast, promotion of Green Mountain Falls began in 1887 as soon as railroad access was assured. Streets were built along with the mandatory real-estate office. The Green Mountain Falls Hotel opened in 1889. A man-made lake featured an island on which a gazebo would be built. Railroad excursions brought visitors, hundreds at a time. Circus entrepreneur P. T. Barnum had a summer home here. Hybrid tents decorated the hillsides: Their canvas tops were removed every autumn and replaced on their log bottoms every spring to prepare for the onslaught of fair-weather visitors. To visit Green Mountain Falls, turn left from US 24 onto Green Mountain Falls Road. The hotel is gone, as are all the grand old Ute Pass hotels. The lake and its gazebo are the most recognizable remnants of the early history of Ute Pass, and the railroad grade is a path on the side of the lake opposite the road. The Church of the Wildwood still incorporates the portion of that structure built in 1889. Return as you came. Make a left turn on US24 and continue west.

Crystola, now just a few commercial buildings at a wide spot in the road, had its unusual origins in the occult. Early settlers were adherents to spiritualism and psychic phenomena, popular around the time of the Civil War. A visiting medium claimed to use his psychic power to discover gold near Crystola in 1897, and investors lost all their money in a scheme than never produced an ounce of the shiny metal.

The valley of Fountain Creek widens and Manitou Park opens to the north. The railroad station here was first called Manitou Park and then Woodland Park. The city of Woodland Park was incorporated in 1890. Dr. William Bell had already constructed a resort near here and other hotels would be built, as Woodland Park was to become the westernmost Ute Pass resort town. Woodland Park was also a sawmill town with five mills turning logs into lumber. Tiny narrow-gauge trains struggled from Manitou Lake bringing logs to the mills. Modern development has been particularly aggressive here, leaving precious few historical landmarks. You might visit the Pikes Peak Museum and the Ute Pass History Park located near the Ute Pass Cultural Center. The museum is operated by the Ute Pass Historical Society whose knowledgeable volunteers can help you with the history of all the towns on Ute Pass.

The first permanent settlers in Teller County chose Divide—the summit of Ute Pass—as their new home in 1870. Soon, lumber and other commerce funneled through town. The railroad arrived in 1887 and remained until 1949. Cattlemen stopped at local false-front saloons to whet their whistles as the mournful whistle of the railroad echoed off the mountains. Not only did the waters divide here; so did the railroad tracks. The Colorado Midland continued west to Grand Junction and the Midland Terminal south to Cripple Creek. Times changed and, by the 1920s, Divide was an agricultural area with lettuce and seed potatoes shipped out on the railroad. Winter ice was harvested in Coulson Lake. Men would cut it into large blocks that were stored in insulated warehouses until needed to cool lettuce on its long journey to market. The railroad depot will be on your left (south) as you enter town but has had an addition that makes it hard to spot. The town's old schoolhouse is on the southwest corner of the intersection of U.S. 24 and Colorado Highway 67.

The Florissant Fossil Beds National Monument is 2.5 miles south of Florissant which is 8 miles west of Divide on US 24 if you are interested and have time. Exhibits and an interpretive trail explain the fossils. The Monument is not part of this journey but has indoor and outdoor exhibits and an extensive trail system.

To continue this journey from Divide, turn south at Colorado 67 toward Cripple Creek. Travel 6 miles to the little that remains of Midland. Midland had a sawmill and was a water stop on the Midland Terminal Railway.

After Midland, Colorado 67 is located atop the railroad grade. You can tell you are driving an old railroad grade by the gentle hills, wide curves, huge earthen fills, deep rocky cuts, and the single-lane Waters Railroad Tunnel (now renamed the Little Ike Tunnel). The road now bypasses the tunnel but when the author first arrived in Colorado, driving through the tunnel involved turning on your headlights, honking your horn, and entering the one-lane railroad tunnel slowly. It is built on a slight curve, so you had to drive part way inside before you could see if anyone had entered from the opposite direction!

There are few structures left at Gillette where the valley opens up. The shops of the Midland Terminal

Railroad were originally here and 1,200 people lived in what turned out to be a particularly frigid valley in a cold land. Gillette is best known for being the site of the only authentic bullfight ever held in the United States. Your route diverges from that of the railway at Gillette.

Bob Womack struck gold in Poverty Gulch in 1890 and the Cripple Creek & Victor Mining District was born. It was Colorado's last major historic gold rush, and peak production occurred a mere decade after first discovery. Three railroads served the five hundred mines, and two trolley lines served fifty-five thousand people in twelve towns. You'll completely circle Gold Hill—actually a substantial stand of mountains—from which wealth was wrested from the

AS YOU NEAR VICTOR, THE LANDSCAPE CHANGES DRAMATICALLY. OPEN-PIT MINING HAS LEFT HUGE PILES OF WASTE ROCK. THIS OPEN-PIT LANDSCAPE VANISHES BY THE TIME YOU REACH HISTORIC VICTOR. *BARNES IAN/SHUTTERSTOCK*

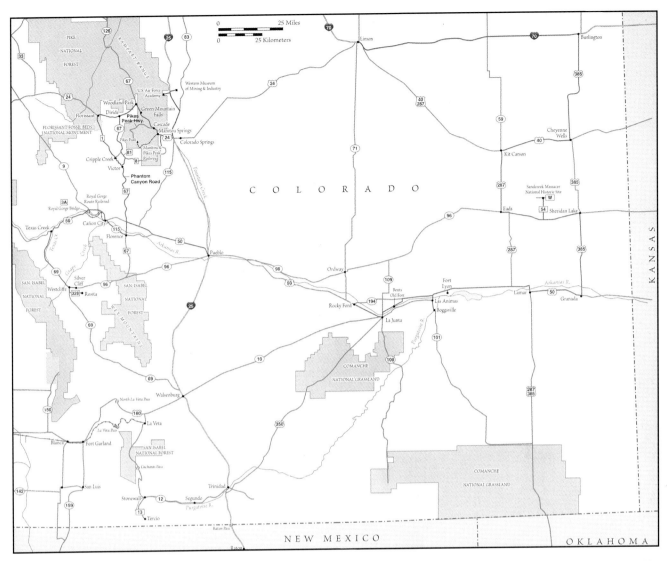

earth. Imagine what you would have seen in 1900 with eight thousand miners working day and night, mills pounding big rocks into small rocks, trains and trolleys squealing around curves, twelve dozen saloons serving a raucous crowd, ladies of the night plying their trade, and families visiting the zoo. It must have been a remarkable sight—an urban industrial landscape 2 miles high!

Crest the hill about 3 miles past Gillette and you will marvel at the spectacular aerial panorama of Cripple Creek. Perhaps you can spot the faint outlines of long-gone city streets in the now-empty fields near town.

As you switchback down the steep hillside that prevented any railroad from entering from this direction, you'll come to the Mollie Kathleen Gold Mine. If time allows, take the informative tour one thousand feet below the earth. The

district's deepest mine was 3,500 feet deep. Near the Mollie Kathleen is the Cripple Creek Heritage Center, featuring aspects of a visitors' center and a media-based museum. Stop here to orient yourself to the district's history.

Cripple Creek was incorporated in 1892 but a great fire destroyed the town just four years later. A majestic town was built on its ashes, and it was the largest city in the mining district and the fourth largest in Colorado in 1900. Just before you reach the historic downtown, the Cripple Creek District Museum will be on your left housed in the multistoried Midland Terminal Railroad depot. It features excellent exhibits on the railroad, mining, and Cripple Creek itself. Once, you could purchase tickets for Paris, France, in this depot, including the steamship coupon!

The very narrow-gauge steam trains of the Cripple Creek & Victor Narrow

Gauge Railroad leave from the Bull Hill Depot, moved here from its original location east of Victor. You'll be treated to an outdoor museum of actual mines, mills, and ghost towns, all interpreted by the train's engineer.

Bennett Street bisects Cripple Creek's historic downtown, which is now filled with new gambling casinos behind the historic facades of original buildings. Brothels were once located on Myers Avenue, a block south of Bennett. One, the 1896 Old Homestead House Museum on Myers Avenue, has an informative tour explaining the "adult" entertainment of historic Cripple Creek. You'll need to make a left turn in Cripple Creek toward Victor.

South of Cripple Creek, you are on the roadbed of the narrow-gauge Florence & Cripple Creek Railroad. The first to arrive in the district in 1894, the Florence & Cripple Creek Railroad

THE ROYAL GORGE BRIDGE, ONE OF THE WORLD'S
HIGHEST SUSPENSION BRIDGES, CROSSES THE
CANYON 956 FEET ABOVE THE ARKANSAS RIVER.
PHOTOTRIPPINGAMERICA/SHUTTERSTOCK

was the first to be abandoned when its owners decided not to rebuild it after a 1912 flood washed away much of the track in Phantom Canyon.

As you near Victor, the landscape changes dramatically, because modern open-pit mining has created huge tailings (waste rock) piles near the highway. The open pit landscape vanishes by the time you reach historic Victor, which retains its nineteenth-century ambiance better any than other large mining town in Colorado. Mine owners lived in Cripple Creek, but many of the mine workers lived in Victor. There are numerous historic buildings and you must spend time walking around town. You can even spend the night in the four-story Victor Hotel, which is beautifully restored down to its bird-cage elevator.

Adventurer and Victor native Lowell Thomas invented travelogues, motion pictures about faraway places, and toured the world presenting them. Magazine editor, radio broadcaster, the very first television newsman, and the

host of two television series, Thomas was a renaissance man. His hometown honors him and recalls its own history at the Victor Lowell Thomas Museum.

Hiking in a heavily mined area is inherently dangerous with thousand-foot-deep shafts perilously close to the surface. You will find an abundance of safe interpretive trails in the Victor area, and you should walk at least one of them. The Independence Mill Site, Battle Mountain, Golden Circle, and Vindicator Valley trails are a few trail options. All are lined with century-old mining artifacts.

The American Eagles Mine is located high above Victor, and its surface plant is open to public inspection. Most of its structures date from 1895, and it is the highest mine in the district at 10,570 feet above sea level. Then as now, the highest mine has the most breathtaking views.

Follow Colorado 67 through Victor. Colorado 67 is also called the Phantom Canyon Road south of Victor. A few turns are required to stay on 67.

Cañon City is built the Shelf Road, then a toll road, to the Cripple Creek & Victor Mining District in 1892. To ensure its share of the riches, Florence constructed the Florence and Cripple Creek Free Road through Phantom Canyon. Florence would win the major portion of trade with the Cripple Creek & Victor Mining District when the Florence and Cripple Creek Railroad was built on the grade of its Free Road in 1894. Smelters were built near Florence to process ore from the Cripple Creek & Victor Mining District. That railroad was washed out by a 1912 flood, never to be rebuilt, and the right-of-way became the Phantom Canyon Road, now a historic byway between Florence and Victor. There are two railroad tunnels, an original steel bridge, and remnants of a few structures along the way.

The second commercial oil field in the United States was discovered near Florence in 1862. Florence became a major center of the nascent petroleum industry as the twentieth century dawned. Later, coal was discovered and mined south of Florence. Short railroads were built to carry coal to a connection with the Denver & Rio Grande Railroad. It is no wonder that downtown Florence is populated with large buildings of brick and stone for prosperity arrived in three forms: oil, gold, and coal. Stop at the Price Pioneer Museum. Florence has an historic downtown, which include shops and restaurants. Take Colorado Highway 115 east from Florence. In Cañon City, turn left (west) at US Highway 50 and left again (south) on third street for the Royal Gorge Route Railroad depot. Instead, you can turn right (north) on third street to arrive at Cañon City's historic downtown on Main Street.

After the Santa Fe Railroad's track blocked the Denver & Rio Grande's track from Raton Pass, the two railroads battled for a route in the bottom of the Royal Gorge. This time the battle was fought with real bullets and famous gunslingers like Bat Masterson. The war ended in a stalemate and a treaty enabled the Denver & Rio Grande to build through the gorge. Ride the passenger train of the Royal Gorge Route Railroad through the 1000-foot-deep, 30-foot-wide slit in the mountains under the Royal Gorge Bridge. Trains depart from the historic Santa Fe depot in Cañon City.

Cañon City was founded in 1860 as a supply center for mining and agriculture. The Museum of Colorado Prisons is housed in the original 1935 Women's Correctional Facility. The first inmate arrived at Cañon City's first prison, the Colorado Territorial Prison, in 1871. The Royal Gorge Regional Museum and History Center is located in the 1927 Municipal Building. The building is on the National Register of Historic Places as is the old downtown of about eighty buildings! On the east side of town on US Highway 50, The Benedictine Holy Cross Abbey was established in 1926. No longer owned by the Benedictines, the Abbey hosts a The Winery at Holy Cross Abbey among several new functions. It is a beautiful historic site worth visiting. Continue west on US Highway 50.

The Royal Gorge Bridge was erected in 1929 to attract tourists, a function it has served admirably since. The suspension bridge is 1,053 feet above the Arkansas River and is owned by Cañon City. A trolley line once connected the bridge site to town. Drive back to US 50 and turn left (west) to reach Texas Creek where you will turn left on Colorado Highway 69 to reach Westcliffe.

The Wet Mountain Valley is sandwiched between the Wet and the Sangre de Cristo mountains. In 1870, you would have heard settlers speaking German at the communal agricultural community of Colfax founded by 357 immigrants from Germany. Though the colony failed, many of the Germans remained to farm or ranch. Other settlers would arrive, but it was the 1870 visit of General William Palmer with his friend Dr. William Bell that would have the most impact on the valley. Bell was so entranced with the area that he purchased a large town site and would later rename it Westcliffe after his hometown in England. Silver mines gave birth to the neighboring town of Rosita whose heydays lasted from 1872 to 1881 when much of the town burned to the ground. Fortunately, silver had already been discovered nearby at Silver Cliff in 1879. Five thousand people called Silver Cliff home just one year later.

Palmer's Denver & Rio Grande Railroad arrived in 1881, building its depot on Dr. Bell's land at Westcliffe, west of existing Silver Cliff. It pays to have powerful friends for Westcliffe became, and still is, the predominant city in the valley. After floods washed out the narrow-gauge track along Grape Creek three times, the railroad threw in the towel in 1890. Mining ceased. Rosita became a ghost town and Silver Cliff almost disappeared as well. Agriculture saved the valley from being abandoned and Westcliffe was the supply center for agriculture. Denver & Rio Grande trains soon arrived again. This time standard-gauge trains whistled into town from Texas Creek until 1937, when the Great Depression silenced those mournful wails.

Drive around Westcliffe and adjacent Silver Cliff (east on Colorado Highway 69.) Both harbor interesting old structures. Westcliffe has the Old School House Museum. The railroad's restored engine house is near the historical Railroad District's interpretive center. Silver Cliff houses its museum in the Silver Cliff Town Hall and Fire Station. There are also a few historic buildings still standing at Rosita. To reach Rosita, drive south of Westcliffe on Colorado 69 for 3.5 miles and turn left on County Road 328 (Rosita Road.) Drive 7 miles east to reach Rosita.

Chapter 2

NEW MEXICO AND ARIZONA

By Jim Hinckley

AS WITH MOST OF ROUTE 66, THE
HIGHWAY IN NEW MEXICO IS BROKEN
AND SEGMENTED WITH LARGE
PORTIONS SERVING AS AN ACCESS
ROAD FOR INTERSTATE 40. HOWEVER,
THE PORTIONS THAT REMAIN ARE
WELL POSTED AND EASILY FOLLOWED.

DOUBLE-6
in the LAND OF
ENCHANTMENT

GLENRIO TO GALLUP

THE BLUE HOLE IN SANTA ROSA, NEW MEXICO, IS
AN APTLY NAMED DESERT OASIS THAT IS POPULAR
WITH PICNICKERS, ROUTE 66 ENTHUSIASTS, AND
SCUBA DIVERS.

The state of New Mexico's motto is The Land of Enchantment. That is also an apt description of a drive across the state from the panhandle of Texas to the Arizona state line on iconic Route 66. Scenic wonder. Tangible links to more than a thousand years of history. A modern, bustling city. Neon-lit nights and starry skies. Route 66 in New Mexico is enchanting, magical, and memorable.

If driving east to west, it all begins with the ghost town of Glenrio that straddles the New Mexico and Texas state line. From its inception in 1905, this dusty village has been unique. It was established as a depot and siding for the Chicago, Rock Island & Gulf Railroad in the heart of a hard scrabble farming and ranching area. Deaf Smith County in Texas was dry. So, the businesses that offered libations were located on the west side of town that happened to be in New Mexico.

Establishment of the Ozark Trails Highway, predecessor to Route 66, in the 1910s fostered establishment of service industries such as garages and service stations. By 1920 the business district included the Glenrio Hotel, a depot, land office, grocery store, hardware store, lumber company, and restaurants. There was even a weekly newspaper, the *Glenrio Tribune*, that was launched in 1910.

The post–World War I economic recession led to a collapse in agricultural prices just as a drought was devastating local farms. Then came the Great Depression and the Dust Bowl. But Glenrio survived, even after the railroad suspended operations and the depot closed because of the ever-increasing flow of traffic on Route 66. What the community couldn't weather was the bypass of Route 66 with completion of the interstate highway in 1975. Within 18 months, only one business remained in operation.

Today Glenrio is a favored photo stop for Route 66 travelers. The remnants of the business district and overgrown four lane highway that was once U.S. 66 were listed in the National Register of Historic Places in 2007. This designation includes sites as well as seventeen buildings such as the State Line Bar, Little Juarez Diner, and a service station. A popular photo op is the Texas Longhorn Motel and Restaurant. During the heyday, west bound travelers saw a sign that read, "Last Motel and Restaurant in Texas." For east bound travelers, the sign read, "First Motel and Restaurant in Texas."

The pavement that once carried Route 66 traffic ends just west of Glenrio. The overgrown and no longer drivable alignment that was the last incarnation of the storied old highway stretches across the high desert plain toward I-40. The older alignment, now a graded gravel road, continues west through the fast fading remnants of Endee, another ghost town, and then into San Jon. As a bit of historic trivia, in 1906 the last use of a horse mounted posse in the state of New Mexico captured a band of rustlers in Endee.

For westbound travelers, the last alignment of Route 66 that dates to the 1950s is accessed via the first I-40 exit in New Mexico. It too can be followed into San Jon but the highlight of this drive is Russell's Truck and Travel Plaza. The outward appearance is that this is a modern full-service truck stop but nestled inside is an expansive (and free) auto museum peppered with relics from Route 66, Glenrio, and Endee.

If you enjoy photographing long closed businesses with ghost signs, take time to explore faded old San Jon.

The road from San Jon to Tucumcari is a glimpse at Route 66 travel in the 1950s. As you start down the canyon west of San Jon watch for the tumble down remains of a service station on the right side of the road. The canopy roof that once shaded the gas pumps is shingled with carefully flattened oil cans!

Tucumcari was severely impacted when the interstate highway bypassed Route 66 that had funneled thousands of cars through town every day. That economic calamity is made manifest in the shuttered motels and truck stops, and by the towering signs that cast long shadows over empty lots. But in recent years, this town began harnessing the international fascination with Route 66 as a catalyst for revitalization and Tucumcari has become famous for the renovated time capsules.

The crown jewel is the 1939 Blue Swallow Motel. The renovated property with its stunning neon signage is one of the most photographed locations on Route 66. Tee Pee Curios is a throwback to the glory days of Route 66, and its restored neon signage is a favored attraction for photographers. Other gems include Pow Wow Restaurant & Lizard Lounge, the 1959 Motel Safari, and the Roadrunner Lodge that the owners have transformed into a touch of "1964 Swank" through an eye for period detail.

Located off Route 66 is the Tucumcari Historical Museum. While it is well worth a visit, the big surprise is Mesalands Community College's Dinosaur Museum. It has been described as a diminutive Smithsonian National Museum of Natural History. And at the convention center on the west side of town is an excellent Route 66 museum.

From Tucumcari to Albuquerque, Route 66 must be enjoyed in segments as it has been bisected by I-40. Nestled around or near exits are remnants of once bustling communities; Montoya, Newkirk, and Cuervo. Each offers a myriad of wonderful photo ops and an opportunity to reflect on what Route 66 meant to these rural villages.

Santa Rosa was also hard hit by the bypass of Route 66, but this town is well worth a stop and a bit of exploration. There are modern motels and restaurants and more than a few treasures. If you make but one stop in Santa Rosa, make it the Blue Hole. Located along the original alignment of Route 66, this vintage roadside park was built around a circular, bell-shaped artesian well with crystal blue waters that have such clarity it is possible to see more than one hundred feet toward the bottom. More than 3,000 gallons of cool, clear water flow from the depths daily. Not surprisingly this is one of the most popular scuba diving locations in the United States.

Before 1937, west of Santa Rosa, Route 66 originally made a long sweeping curve north to Santa Fe and then turned due south toward Albuquerque. I will share highlights of that alignment in the Route 32 section.

West of Santa Rosa, almost all the way to Moriarty, Route 66 is decimated. Scattered here and there are short segments and remnants that hint of better times. The innovative Route 66 Navigation app (route66navigation. com) or *EZ66 Guide for Travelers* map book by Jerry McClanahan are your best options to find these tarnished treasures.

Moriarty is amply peppered with restaurants, motels, and photo ops. But the towns treasure is the Sunset Motel, a true gem. This meticulously maintained property, with original signage, opened in 1959. It is the only 1950s motel in the hands of the original family anywhere on Route 66. Their pride in ownership is evident.

Following Route 66 down Tijeras Canyon has an increasingly urban feel as you draw closer to Albuquerque. Still, the sharp-eyed traveler will glimpse vestiges from the highway's glory days nestled among the modern fast-food restaurants, strip malls, supermarkets, convenience stores, and car lots.

Albuquerque is a modern metropolis with the traffic to prove it. But, from a Route 66 perspective, it is unique as the highway corridor is as it was after 1937: East Central Avenue and West Central Avenue on the other side of the Rio Grande and up Nine Mile Hill. From beginning to end, aside from the crush of traffic, this drive is an exciting

THE TRADING POSTS AT CONTINENTAL DIVIDE, NEW MEXICO, ARE A THROWBACK TO THE GLORY DAYS OF ROUTE 66.

blend of original businesses, repurposed historic buildings, restored businesses including motels, and historic business districts, some of which date to the late eighteenth century. And with the shortest of detours, you can enjoy exciting experiences such as the Sandia Peak Tramway.

Spanish explorers that arrived at this location on the Rio Grande in 1540 noted the ruins of a Native American community at the site. The modern incarnation of Albuquerque dates to a survey and development of a settlement plan in 1706. The Old Town Albuquerque district encompasses about ten blocks of historic adobe buildings along Route 66. On the north side of the plaza is the San Felipe de Neri Church, the oldest building in the city, which was built in 1793. Surrounding the church, original buildings house an array of galleries, shops, and fascinating restaurants.

West of Old Town, at 3916 Central Ave SW, is a seedy looking liquor store that hides a secret—Monte Carlo Liquors & Steak House. Indicative of the restaurant's local popularity is the

difficulty in finding a parking space and the recommendations that reservations be made. The entrance is through the liquor store and down a dark narrow hallway past the coolers. Excellent food and unique ambiance are always a winner in my book.

Another attraction of note is the Albuquerque Biological Park that is accessed via Central Avenue, Route 66. Located on the banks of the Rio Grande, the complex consists of the ABQ BioPark Zoo, Botanic Garden, Aquarium, and Tingley Beach.

Established in 1927, the zoo houses more than 900 animals from around the world in carefully crafted natural habitats. Many of these animals have been part of a successful captive breeding program that has served as a template for other zoos. The Botanic Garden that opened in 1996 was recently expanded to thirty-two acres of exhibits. One of the most popular exhibits at the garden is the BUGarium, the largest display of insects and arthropods in the country. Also established in 1996 is the ABQ BioPark Aquarium, that includes the Shark Reef

Café with views into the 285,000-gallon ocean tank. Tingley Beach consists of three fishing ponds and a mile-long walking trail that loops around the ponds and provides access to the Rio Grande. Pedal boat rentals are available during the months of summer.

West of the Rio Grande, the Central Avenue corridor is a bit more tarnished and gritty than on the east end, and a surprising number of motels, restaurants, and garages from the glory days of Route 66 have survived into the modern era. This means there are lots of photo ops, but use discretion as the area is a bit rough around the edges. There are also some wonderful time capsules that I highly recommend such as the Western View Steak House and Coffee Shop with its 1950s signage and excellent food.

West of Albuquerque the interstate highway again intrudes on the timeless feel of a drive on Route 66. Still, there are portals into that lost world such as the Enchanted Trails Trading Post & RV Park and the bypassed, steel truss Rio Puerco Bridge.

At exit 117 you can again begin the
Route 66 experience and follow the
old road through a storybook land of
colorful buttes and rock formations.
It should be noted that the drive
through the villages of Laguna and New
Laguna are on Indian reservations. Be
respectful and be aware that there are
some restrictions on photographs taken
without permits.

In this part of New Mexico, Route 66
is no mere highway, it is a portal that
links the past with the present. As an
example, people have been living at the
site of Laguna for at least seven hundred
years. A slight detour south from Paraje
on highway 23 will take you to the
pueblo of Acoma perched on a mesa
high above the valley. This is the oldest
continuously inhabited community in
the United States. Archaeologists have
documented occupation since at least
1200 C.E.

A Technicolor wonderland of
mountains, canyons, buttes, and mesas
frame places like Budville, a wide spot
in the road that provided services to

Route 66 travelers for decades before
the murder of the owner. Just to the
west of Budville, the original alignment
of the highway loops through Cubero
with its adobe ruins that date to the early
nineteenth century. Villa de Cubero is
a small rural store and long shuttered
motel that was once an oasis for the rich
and famous including Lucille Ball, Desi
Arnaz, and Ernest Hemingway.

A travel point of note needs to be
made about the I-40 underpass to the
west of McCarty. It is one vehicle wide
and clearance is only 13' 6". And after
a rain, standing water can be deep. It is
often muddy. So, plan accordingly.

The town of Grants was dealt a
double blow economically. As with
other communities, the Route 66
bypass hit service industry businesses
hard. Grants was also at the center of a
uranium mining boom, and when this
came to an end, a downward economic
spiral commenced in earnest. A highly
recommended stop in this historic
old town is the New Mexico Mining
Museum. In addition to exhibits

that chronicle the city's history and its association with Route 66, there is an excellent interactive exhibit, in the basement, that mimics mine exploration.

To the west of Grants are tangible links to the pre-interstate highway era including trading posts and signs with photo ops that designate this point to be the continental divide. Authentic Native American trading posts and roadside stands to sell produce or jewelry have been enticing travelers since the era of the National Old Trails Road, predecessor to Route 66, and that tradition continues to this day. Unfortunately, west from the Continental Divide to exit 36 the interstate highway again becomes the only option.

Gallup is a delight. It is a modern community with all expected amenities as well as restaurants that date to the 1950s, authentic trading posts, a business district rich with early twentieth-century architecture, and the magical El Rancho Hotel. Promoted as the "World's Largest Ranch House" after opening in 1937, the hotel with its rustic frontier styled lobby quickly became the home away from home for Hollywood celebrities.

The hotel was built by R.E. Griffith, brother to movie mogul D.W. Griffith. From 1940 to 1964 eighteen major motion pictures were filmed in the area and the hotel served as the headquarters for film companies. Celebrities frequented the bar and restaurant which

added to its allure for 66 travelers. The upper mezzanine in the lobby serves as a gallery for autographed pictures that represent more than sixty years of Hollywood history. Here is an historic tidbit: John Wayne kept a suite next to the bar on retainer.

The restaurant is highly recommended just as it was in the AAA Western Accommodations Directory published in 1954. Aside from traditional American fare, the menu is filled with hunger inducing offerings including traditional dishes, authentic New Mexico dinners, and even regional traditional Native American meals.

An overnight stay is an unforgettable experience. There is, however, a caveat. The hotel is clean and well maintained

THE GLOW OF NEON ALONG ROUTE 66 IN SANTA
ROSA, NEW MEXICO, MAY HAVE DIMMED BUT
SCATTERED THROUGH TOWN ARE HINTS THAT A
RENAISSANCE IS BREWING.

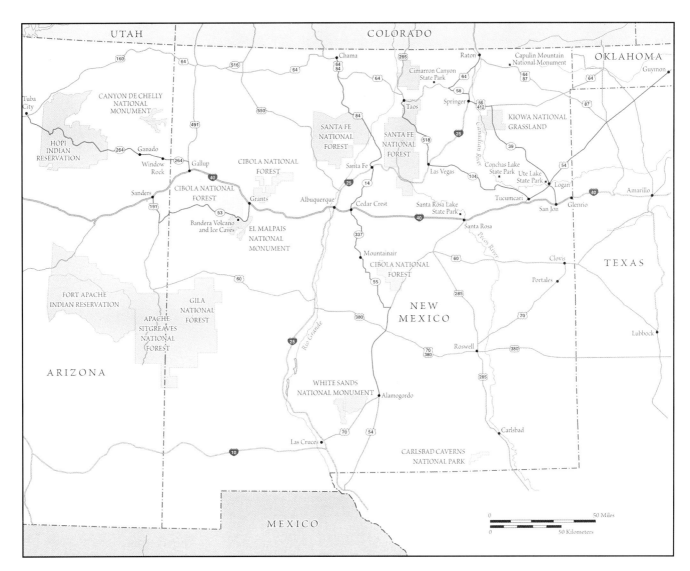

but it is old. In the 1940s this was a five-star resort, but times change. The rooms are small, and the bathrooms almost claustrophobic. In essence this hotel is a true time capsule.

I have a couple of other recommendations to make that will enhance a visit to Gallup. One is Earl's Family Restaurant, a well-preserved roadside relic that opened in 1947. Aside from excellent food, what makes this place special is the traders. Just as in the pre-interstate highway era, Native American traders sell their wares outside on the patio. And inside, unless you make a request, traders will come by your table offering kachinas, jewelry, and other handicrafts.

The other is Richardson Trading Company that opened in 1913. This is not a tourist centered business with a blending of souvenirs, trinkets, and quality merchandise. This is an authentic trading post that hearkens back to the western frontier. This one family owned business has been providing a valued service to members of the Navajo, Hopi, and Zuni tribes for more than a century.

The drive from Gallup to the Arizona state line is short but scenic. Unfortunately, much of it is on a state highway as Route 66 was buried under I-40. Still, from border to border a drive across New Mexico on Route 66 will leave no doubt as to why New Mexico is promoted as the Land of Enchantment.

By Jim Hinckley

An ANCIENT LAND

TUCUMCARI TO ALBUQUERQUE

HEAD NORTHWEST OUT OF TUCUMCARI ON STATE ROUTE 104, A 106-MILE DRIVE TO LAS VEGAS. THERE, CONTINUE NORTH ON STATE ROUTE 518 TO TAOS, 77 MILES. WITH THE EXCEPTION OF SCENIC HIGHWAY 104 TO LAS VEGAS, THIS DRIVE FOLLOWS THE ORIGINAL ALIGNMENT OF ROUTE 66 THAT IS ALSO THE COURSE FOR THE NATIONAL OLD TRAILS ROAD AND HISTORIC SANTA FE TRAIL.

LOOKING FROM THE PLAZA DOWN BRIDGE STREET THE SENSE OF HISTORY IS ALMOST PALPABLE IN THE ORIGINAL LAS VEGAS.

AT THE END OF THE SANTA FE TRAIL TODAY, SANTA FE, NEW MEXICO

2305-30

The drive from Tucumcari, through the original Las Vegas and old Santa Fe, and into Albuquerque exemplifies the best of the great American road trip. Stunning scenery, breath taking vistas, historic sites, Route 66, and timeless villages that seem suspended in time are but a few of the highlights. It begins at the intersection of Tucumcari Boulevard (Route 66) and South 1st Street, highway 104.

First, there is a cruise through the original business district, past the recently renovated depot, home to the Tucumcari Railroad Museum, and then into a New Mexico landscape that seems unchanged since the expeditions of Coronado in 1540. The first leg of this adventure is a drive of 110 scenic miles from Tucumcari to Las Vegas.

As with Route 66, this highway gently twists and turns across the high desert, through nearly forgotten towns with faded links to better times, and over gently rolling hills. Shortly past the oasis of Lake Conchas and the nearly empty wide spot in the road that is Trementina, the highway begins a steep climb up the face of the Canadian Escarpment. Make use of the scenic overlooks and pullouts to savor the awe-inspiring beauty that stretches to the horizons.

After a drive that seems timeless, the appearance of Las Vegas and the traffic of I25 is almost startling. To the left, across the interstate highway, stands the imposing Castañeda Hotel, a bridge between the past and present and a hint of the wonders awaiting discovery in the original Las Vegas.

After a slumber of nearly sixty years, this venerable hotel was recently renovated and is now a showpiece of the city once again. The Castañeda was built in 1898 and was the first Fred Harvey railroad hotel. A 500-foot-long portico that wraps around the entire east facade and embraces the courtyard gives the landmark an inviting appeal. Blurring the line between past and present is the Amtrak station next door and the trains that roll past the hotel daily.

The historic significance of the property cannot be understated. The Castañeda was designed by Frederick Roehrig, a prominent Pasadena architect, in a Mission Revival style. It served as a template for the first-generation Harvey properties. It was here that the Harvey Girls program was first tested, and directly across the street the beautiful Rawlings Building originally served as a dormitory for the Las Vegas Harvey Girls. On June 24, 1899, Teddy Roosevelt hosted the first

reunion of the Rough Riders at this hotel and led a parade through town.

The surrounding district is amply peppered with architectural masterpieces that date to the late nineteenth century and early twentieth century. Until the late 1960s, this was New Las Vegas. A mile to the east was old Las Vegas. That district is even more amazing. Bridge Street leading to the plaza is lined with mid to late nineteenth-century buildings. Towering over the shaded plaza on the Santa Fe Trail is the renovated 1882 Plaza Hotel. Still standing is a storefront building where on August 15, 1846, Brigadier General Stephen Kearny stood on the parapet and announced to a crowd on the plaza that this was now American territory.

Las Vegas is a small town with a population of just over 13,000 people. And yet there are 900 buildings listed on the National Register of Historic Places. To get the best out of a Las Vegas visit, I suggest exploring it on foot.

A few short miles west of Las Vegas you can again begin a Route 66 adventure, albeit in pieces. This is the pre-1937 alignment of that highway as well as the course for the National Old

Trails Road and Santa Fe Trail. The sense of history on the drive to Santa Fe is almost palpable. Just consider the village of Tecolote, the first "town" you will encounter.

Officially the village dates to 1824 even though farming by immigrants commenced earlier. On the plaza is a small adobe church of indefinite age but it was noted in the diary of William Anderson Thornton, a member of a military expedition that encamped here in the summer of 1855.

To access San Jose, a very slight detour is needed. This village also feels ancient. Initial settlement and farming along the Pecos River commenced in 1803. The little church has cast its shadow over the Santa Fe Trail, National Old Trails Road and Route 66. And at the far end of town is a long-closed single lane steel truss bridge that spans the Pecos River. It was built in 1921 and carried Route 66 traffic until 1937.

But even a village that was founded two centuries ago is considered modern in this part of New Mexico. Located

on highway 63, originally U.S. 66, is Pecos National Historic Park. Here, framed by the stunning Sangre de Cristo Mountains are the towering remnants of Pecos Pueblo, a city known to Spanish conquistadors as Cicuye. Established around 1100 C.E., over a period of several hundred years, the village became the hub of a vast trading network. Archeologists estimated that the five storied complexes were once home to a population of more than 2,000 people.

Spanish cartographers traveling with Francisco Coronado in 1540 noted that it was the largest city they had encountered north of Mexico. The impressive adobe ruins of Mission Nuestra Señora de los Ángeles de Porciúncula de los Pecos built in the early seventeenth century are also preserved at the site.

Another part of the park is the Forked Lightning Ranch, a cattle ranch established in the 1920s by Tex Austin, a famous producer of rodeos. The ranch headquarters were originally

the Kozlowski Stage Stop and Tavern, a stop on the Santa Fe Trail. During the American Civil War, Union forces encamped at this location before the pivotal Battle of Glorieta Pass.

A few miles to the west, before it becomes necessary to join I25 for the drive into Santa Fe, there is a nondescript adobe building built so close to the highway it almost touches the guard rail. This is the last vestige of the Pigeon Ranch that was built as a hostelry in the shadow of Glorieta Pass on the Santa Fe Trail. During the Battle of Glorieta Pass in 1862, it served as a field hospital. In the era of the National Old Trails Road during the dawning of automobile tourism, it was an oasis as well as a tourist attraction. Emily Post and Edsel Ford both stopped here during

THE IMPOSING RUINS AT PECOS NATIONAL HISTORICAL PARK FRAMED BY QUINTESSENTIAL WESTERN LANDSCAPES PRESENT A SENSE OF TIMELESSNESS.

OLD PIGEON RANCH ON SANTA FE TRAIL, NEW MEXICO.

IN THE ERA OF THE NATIONAL OLD TRAILS ROAD, THE VENERABLE OLD PIGEON RANCH WAS AN OASIS AS WELL AS A ROADSIDE ATTRACTION.

their trips to California in 1915. Hidden from view on the opposite of the road is an old stone well. Legend has it that it was used by Coronado. There is not historic support for the story but there is evidence that it was in use during the eighteenth century.

The historic heart of Santa Fe is a labyrinth of twisting narrow streets. Don't let this discourage you from exploring a fascinating and dynamic city that was established in 1610. But this too is a recent chapter as it was built on the ruins of a large and ancient pueblo.

Vestiges from centuries of history abound, many are private homes while others serve as restaurants just as they have for more than a century. As an example, the De Vargas Street House is believed to be the oldest building in the city. It dates to the early seventeenth century. The Mission San Miguel is the oldest continuously operated church in the United States. It was built between 1610 and 1628, burned during the

Pueblo Revolt of 1680 and rebuilt in 1710.

The Palace of the Governors, now a museum complex, is another link to the city's rich history. Erected about 1610, it remains as the oldest public building constructed by European settlers in the continental United States. It served as the home for the governor and the seat of government for the Spanish, Mexicans, and Americans until 1907.

For the Route 66 enthusiasts, Santa Fe is home to a special treasure, the magical El Rey Court, originally El Rey Inn, built in 1937. Renovated and transformed into an 80-room complex through the combing of two vintage motels, this is truly an urban oasis. The shade dappled landscaped grounds also serve as a bird sanctuary.

Originally Route 66 followed much of the Spanish Colonial era El Camino Real de Tierra Adentro from Santa Fe into Albuquerque. Here too the sense of history is palpable. About 3 miles

from the village of Domingo on Route 66 that dates to 1883 is the Domingo Pueblo established in 1770. San Felipe was an ancient village when Francisco Coronado arrived in 1540. The post office in Algodones was established in 1855. This early alignment of Route 66 enters Albuquerque on the Fourth Street corridor that is lined a with a cornucopia of architectural styles from various periods of time. These include a café that dates to 1926, and even a vintage Hudson dealership.

This drive is a unique and rare adventure as it is a rich tapestry of history, scenic wonder, the vibrancy of a modern city, fine dining opportunities, and historic hotels. For that reason, it rates as one of my favorite road trips.

By Jim Hinckley

FROM I-40 WEST OF ASH FORK TAKE
THE CROOKTON ROAD EXIT. FOLLOW
ROUTE 66 (ARIZONA HIGHWAY 66) WEST
TO KINGMAN, WHERE IT BECOMES
ANDY DEVINE AVENUE. THE ROUTE
SOUTHWEST THROUGH KINGMAN, AS
WELL AS TO GOLDROAD, OATMAN, AND
THROUGH THE TOPOCK MARSHES, IS
WELL POSTED AS ROUTE 66.

AMERICA'S MAIN *Street*

ROUTE 66 FROM ASH FORK TO TOPOCK

RESTORATION OF THE OLD TRAILS GARAGE FAÇADE
IS BUT ONE MANIFESTATION OF THE RENAISSANCE
THAT IS TRANSFORMING THE HISTORIC HEART OF
KINGMAN, ARIZONA.

For an international legion of Route 66 enthusiasts, this is the Holy Grail of a Route 66 adventure. With the exception of a short segment between Ash Fork, Arizona, and Crookton Road, the entire drive is on Route 66. This is the longest uninterrupted segment of the iconic highway remaining, a scenic drive that is promoted as 160 Miles of Smiles.

Ash Fork is located at the confluence of the three tributaries of Ash Creek, a favored camping site for early explorers including Lt. Edward Beale and his famous camel caravan, Kit Carson and Bill Williams, a legendary mountain man. The town dates to the establishment of a railroad construction camp in 1880. In 1895 the town's prominence grew with completion of a rail line to Phoenix that made Ash Fork an important junction in northern Arizona.

The town was dealt several blows in the 1970s from which it never recovered. The downward spiral commenced in 1968 with the razing of the Escalante, a stunning Harvey House that was built in 1907. This was linked with the Santa Fe Railroad relocating operations. Then came two fires that swept through the historic district, one in 1977 and one in 1978. Finally, in 1979, I-40 completed the bypass of the community and in an instant the endless flow of Route 66 traffic through town stopped.

Still, the old town is well worth more than a simple drive through. Historic relics and photo ops abound, there is a first-rate museum and even a couple of surprisingly good restaurants. You can even enjoy superb barbecue and belly up to the bar in an authentic frontier era saloon masked with a 1950s facade.

I-40 is the only option on a west bound drive but that intrusion into the illusion that it is 1960, 1950, or even 1930 is brief. Exit at Crookton Road which is Route 66. A bit of a tip, before continuing to Seligman and Kingman, cross over I-40 and continue east on the broken asphalt of Route 66 to the picturesque 1923 Partridge Creek Bridge. This is a wonderful photo op.

After a visit to the venerable old bridge, head into Seligman on Route 66. The traffic is light to nonexistent, and the landscape bisected by the old road is quintessential western just as seen in countless Technicolor cinematic classics. It is a relaxing drive that stands in stark contrast to a drive on I-40.

Even though to follow Route 66 from Kingman to Seligman is 20 miles longer on the old road, if my schedule allows, I prefer this drive over the interstate in any season.

Seligman is another western frontier railroad and cattle town that was decimated by the Route 66 bypass. But here business owners led by Angel Delgadillo, the tenacious barber whose family came to town from Mexico after WWI, banded together and fought back. They established a cooperative partnership with people in neighboring communities and launched the Historic Route 66 Association of Arizona, petitioned the state for signage, had the highway designated a scenic byway, and kicked off the annual Route 66 Fun Run that now attracts participants from throughout the world.

As a result, the town is a delightful blending of authentic Route 66 and rough and tumble western ranch town with a hint of Disneyland. Over the years Angel has come to be an international celebrity for Route 66 enthusiasts and

so his barbershop and gift shop is a major destination. Often there are tour buses parked out front, and motorcycles are lined up across the street as people stop to pay homage, get a handshake, or maybe even get a shave.

Seligman is best enjoyed on foot, easy to do as it is only a few dozen blocks from end to end. The Snow Cap Drive-in has been entertaining visitors with quirky fun and providing good basic burgers and such since the early 1950s. By comparison the Road Kill Café that opened about 25 years ago is a relatively recent phenomena but its one of a kind menu with offerings such as Splatter Platter and Rigor Mortis Tortoise, excellent food, smiling waitresses, unique ambiance, well stocked gift shop, and a front row seat to Route 66 make it a popular stop.

Likewise, with West Side Lilo's that is owned and managed by Lilo and her family. The outward appearance is that this is a classic small-town roadside diner. But on Route 66 looks can be deceiving. Lilo hales from Wiesbaden,

Germany and so the menu is a rich blending of freshly made cakes and pies, tasty traditional America dishes such as chicken fried steaks and authentic German meals.

West of Seligman, Route 66 crosses the Aubry Valley named after François Xavier Aubry, a legendary French-Canadian explorer and adventurer that pioneered the Santa Fe Trail trade and mapped routes across the desert southwest to California. The wide valley is the home to cattle ranches, herds of pronghorn antelope, prairie dogs, and the black footed ferret. Long freight trains cutting across the valley and vestiges of more than a century of railroad history with the colorful mountains as a backdrop ensure plenty of stops for photos.

Scattered all along the highway are vestiges of earlier alignments of Route 66 and even the National Old Trails Road and forgotten businesses. One of these was Hyde Park, a complex of cabins, a store, garage, and service station. Now less than ruins in the

SELIGMAN IS BEST ENJOYED ON FOOT, WHICH IS EASY TO DO AS IT IS ONLY A FEW DOZEN BLOCKS FROM END TO END.

ASH FORK IS THE SELF-PROCLAIMED FLAGSTONE CAPITAL OF THE WORLD AND THAT IS EVIDENCED WITH A DRIVE THROUGH THE HISTORIC BUSINESS DISTRICT.

NATIONAL OLD TRAILS HIGHWAY, NEAR KINGMAN, ARIZ.

brush before the interstate highway, this roadside stop was promoted with signs up and down Route 66 that read, "Park Your Hide Tonight at Hyde Park."

Grand Canyon Caverns mirrors the entire evolution of Route 66. It was discovered in 1927 and in the early years was as rough as the road itself. Access to the caverns was with use of a winch, rope, and bucket, a device that the owners privately called dope on a rope. In the late 1930s wooden ladders and a swinging bridge made access easier. As a bit of trivia, the materials for this update were salvaged from the Hoover dam construction site.

After the war, when tourism and traffic along Route 66 became a tsunami, the caverns went through an almost never-ending series of transitions. Paved trails and an elevator were added as was a truck stop with service station, motel with swimming pool, and a gift shop and two restaurants. It was the second most visited attraction in the state of Arizona. As a result, Route 66 in front of the caverns was transformed into a four-lane divided highway. Between Albuquerque and Los Angeles this was the only four-lane section of Route 66 outside of urban areas.

With the bypass of Route 66 in the late 1970s, business plummeted. In two years, the caverns experienced an almost 90% decline in visitors and so a downward spiral commenced. About 20 years ago, passionate new owners tapped into the Route 66 renaissance and like the mythical Phoenix the caverns were reborn. The main restaurant was fully restored to its 1964 appearance, and another restaurant was added in the caverns. The motel and swimming pool were refurbished, an RV park was added, and new tours ensured the natural wonder could be enjoyed by everyone. Today the caverns can be explored on a lengthy paved trail but there is also a wheelchair accessible option as well as an actual spelunking tour.

From the caverns Route 66 continues west over rolling hills peppered with juniper and cedar trees before dropping down a steep grade into Peach Springs, the headquarters for the Hualapai Tribe. As you begin the descent, notice the stunning view to the north.

Peach Springs retains a few forlorn vestiges of its association with Route 66, and even the National Old Trails Road. But there is also the modern and pleasant Hualapai Lodge with a superb restaurant. My suggestion, the beef stew or Hualapai tacos.

I would be remiss if I did not mention a unique detour and a one-of-a-kind opportunity, Diamond Creek Road. This is the only road that allows for vehicular access to the Colorado River at the bottom of the Grand Canyon. During the era of the National Old Trails Road, this was such a popular side trip a small rustic hotel was built near the river. Access requires a tribal permit but that can be obtained at the lodge. You can also check on road conditions as this is a gravel road and there are no services available.

The next vestige of civilization on the westward trip along Route 66 is what remains of Truxton. The town that was wholly dependent on Route 66 traffic dates to the early 1950s. The last operating business is a service station and garage. In essence it is a ghost town of long closed cafes and motels.

A few miles (kilometers) further and the highway drops into Truxton Canyon, and a stunning setting of buttes, mesas, and rock formations. Here Route 66 and the railroad are squeezed into a narrow confine before the canyon opens into the Hualapai Valley near Hackberry. Tangible links to more than a century of Arizona history and a new attraction of note are counted among the highlights.

VESTIGES OF FORMER GLORY ABOUND IN THE LONG-
SHUTTERED HOTEL BEALE IN KINGMAN, ARIZONA.

In 1936, at the bottom of canyon near Valentine, the last section of Route 66 was paved making this an all-weather highway from Chicago to Los Angeles.

Attractions abound on this section of Route 66. The Crozier Canyon Ranch, private property, dates to the late nineteenth century. Before 1937 when a flood forced realignment of Route 66, it was also a resort with a restaurant, swimming pool, cabins, and bus stop. Keepers of the Wild is a walkthrough wildlife park of world renown. The Hackberry General Store built in the 1930s has been transformed into a caricature of the roadside business that once lined Route 66. Today the store and its gift shop are counted as a must stop location for Route 66 enthusiasts. The long-abandoned hulking two-story school building near Valentine is a remnant from the Truxton Canyon Indian Agency School complex built in 1903.

Directly to the south of the Hackberry General Store, across the railroad tracks, is the town of Hackberry, now less than a wide spot in the road. The National Old Trails Road and the original alignment of Route 66 followed a course along the village's central street. Before that this was the center of area mining and ranching, and for a brief moment around 1885, the town was considered to serve as the Mohave County seat.

Just as you enter the Hualapai Valley, a strange, seemingly out of place Easter Island styled head appears. This is Antares Point, a mid-1960s service station and restaurant complex that is now home to sculpturer Gregg Arnold, creator of Giganticus Headicus.

Before entering Kingman, you will pass the Kingman Airport and Industrial Park. Once again, I suggest the slightest of detours, as during WWII this was the site of the Kingman Army Airfield, one of the largest flexible gunnery schools in the country. Nestled among the new factories and manufacturing facilities are several tangible links to that aviation history including hangars and a rare control tower. And in the terminal, a repurposed building from the old airfield, there is an excellent diminutive diner.

In Kingman, Route 66 is signed as Andy Devine Avenue, a hint of the

city's rich Hollywood history. Andy Devine, a character actor that appeared in more than 500 motion pictures from the 1920s into the 1960s, hosted a pioneering children's television program in the early 1950s, and starred in several episodes of popular television programs including *Twilight Zone*, grew up in Kingman. Thomas Devine, his father, was the owner and proprietor of the Hotel Beale. In 1955, the television program *This Is Your Life* profiled Andy Devine. As a special surprise it was announced that Front Street, Route 66, would be renamed Andy Devine Avenue.

Route 66 in Kingman is bordered by an interesting swirl of the old, the modern, masquerading time capsules, and historic landmarks. Vintage motels transformed into low rent apartments give way to bustling truck stops, modern motels, and fast-food restaurants as you draw closer to the I-40 interchange.

Several years ago, the World Monuments Fund designated Route 66 motels as the most endangered

mid-twentieth- century commercial properties in the United States. Scarcer still are prewar auto courts. But the rarest motels of all are those that were listed in the *Negro Motorist Green Book*. Kingman has more vintage motels than any community on Route 66.

The Ramada Inn originally opened in 1964 as a Holiday Inn with a restaurant. The Quality Inn also opened in 1964 but ironically it was originally a Ramada Inn. The Siesta Motel, now apartments, opened in 1929. The Hilltop Motel with original signage that opened in 1955 is undergoing a complete renovation. The El Trovatore Motel and Arcadia Lodge, both featured in the Directory of Motor Courts and Cottages published by AAA in 1940, are still existent but the Arcadia is now an apartment complex.

When it comes to rarity, the crown jewel of these vintage motels is the White Rock Court. Dating to 1936, this auto court was the only motel in Kingman that was listed in the *Negro Motorist Green Book*.

A NEIGHBORHOOD BAR BUILT IN AN OLD WOODEN BOXCAR IS A TANGIBLE LINK TO SELIGMAN'S RAILROAD AND FRONTIER HISTORY.

DATING TO 1923, THE PICTURESQUE PARTRIDGE CREEK IS MAROONED ON AN ALIGNMENT OF ROUTE 66 SEVERED BY I-40.

The historic business district was devastated by the bypass of Route 66, but in recent years it has experienced a slowly evolving renaissance, especially on Beale Street one block north of Route 66. The historic Hotel Beale and Brunswick Hotel on Andy Devine Avenue remain shuttered, and yet one block away there is a thriving nightlife of art galleries, eclectic shops, award winning microbreweries, wine bars, and a variety of excellent restaurants.

For Route 66 enthusiasts, the west end of that highway in Kingman is a destination. Locomotive Park with its massive vintage steam locomotive has been a restful oasis for travelers since the late 1950s. Mr. D'z Route 66 Diner is a true landmark in the era of Route 66 renewal but the colorful café is actually an authentic time capsule. It opened in 1939 as Kimo (Ki for Kingman, Mo for Mohave County) Café. Next door is Dunton Motors Dream Machines, a vintage car museum and sales facility housed in a 1946 Ford dealership.

The Powerhouse Visitor Center was built before 1910 as a power generating station. It remained in operation until completion of Hoover Dam. Today the renovated property houses the gift shop for the Historic Route 66 Association of Arizona, the Kingman tourism office, an award-winning Route 66 museum, and the world's only electric vehicle museum. And directly across the park is the Mohave Museum of History & Arts.

From Kingman the old highway cut into the rock face twists and turns through a picturesque canyon that is shared with the railroad, and on the canyon floor, the first alignment of Route 66 that was also the National Old Trails Road. Of particular note are the railroad bridges still adorned with the old Santa Fe railroad logo that appear in photo post cards from the 1920s.

After crossing under I-40 that was laid over the post 1952 alignment of Route 66, the highway sweeps across the Sacramento Valley toward the imposing escarpment of the Black

Mountains. Arguably the drive though these rugged mountains and then down to the desert oasis of the Colorado River is the most beautiful portion of Route 66 between Chicago and Santa Monica.

It is not for the faint of heart as here you will find the steepest grades and sharpest curves anywhere on Route 66, and the road is narrow with few guardrails. You will also find stunning views, time capsules, tumble down ruins, the ghost town of Oatman turned caricature of the Old West mining town where burros roam free on the streets, and the raw beauty of the Havasu National Wildlife Refuge on the Colorado River.

The 160 miles of smiles that is Route 66 in western Arizona is no mere road trip. It is an adventure, an unforgettable blending of the past, present, and future.

ESTABLISHED IN 1926, COOL SPRINGS FRAMED BY STUNNING BACKDROPS IS A FAVORITE STOP FOR THE MODERN ROUTE 66 TRAVELER.

GRAND CANYON CAVERNS WEST OF SELIGMAN, ARIZONA, IS A TANGIBLE LINK TO THE ERA OF FAMILY VACATIONS IN STATION WAGONS, "I LIKE IKE" BUTTONS, AND TAILFINS.

THE VIEWS FROM THE PRE-1952 ALIGNMENT OF
ROUTE 66 IN SITGREAVES PASS IS AWE INSPIRING.

FOR TRAVELERS ON THE NATIONAL OLD TRAILS
ROAD AND ROUTE 66, TOPOCK ON THE COLORADO
RIVER WAS A TRUE DESERT OASIS. TODAY THE
RESORT AT TOPOCK IS A DESTINATION.

By Jim Hinckley

BEGIN IN KINGMAN AT THE INTERSECTION OF STOCKTON HILL ROAD AND ANDY DEVINE AVENUE. FOLLOW THE FORMER NORTH TO THE JUNCTION WITH PIERCE FERRY ROAD. CONTINUE NORTH ON PIERCE FERRY ROAD TOWARD MEADVIEW. JUST SOUTH OF MEADVIEW, TURN RIGHT ONTO DIAMOND BAR ROAD AND FOLLOW THE SIGNS TO GRAND CANYON WEST.

The
ARIZONA
COAST

KINGMAN TO GRAND CANYON WEST

THE RESTAURANT AT GRAND CANYON WESTERN RANCH WAS ONCE THE HOME OF PIONEERING ARIZONA RANCHER TAP DUNCAN.

This is a loop drive that might be considered a sampler of the very best that Arizona has to offer. Jaw dropping scenic wonders, historic sites, vast panoramic landscapes, and the Grand Canyon as it can only be experienced at Grand Canyon West are a few of the highlights.

It kicks off at the intersection of Stockton Hill Road (named for an old nineteenth-century mining camp) and Andy Devine Avenue (Route 66) in Kingman, Arizona. The first miles of this drive are through modern urban sprawl and suburbia framed by the foothills of the picturesque Cerbat Mountains. But don't rush this section of the drive (even if traffic allows that) as there is a little gem on Northern Avenue just one block from Stockton Hill Road.

Considering the fact that it is sort of out of the way and is located more than 5 miles from the highway, Victoria's Sugar Shack has proven to be surprisingly popular with Route 66 travelers as evidenced by a door visitors are encouraged to sign. There are signatures and notes by people from Germany, the Netherlands, and throughout the United States. The draw is the stunning array of fresh baked pies, pastries, and breads, and European type coffee all served in a setting that encourages the guests to sit, savor, and visit.

As Stockton Hill Road continues north from Kingman, it hugs the Cerbat Mountains that stand in stark contrast to the wide Hualapai Valley. Until quite recently this was a stark desert valley dominated by Red Lake, a dusty dry lakebed. Now, with large scale commercial drilling, it is being transformed into a green agricultural paradise.

At Pierce Ferry Road, highway 25, the road enters a large forest to Joshua Trees that appear as though they have been lifted from a Dr. Seuss book. Needless to say, this forest makes for unique photo opportunities, especially at sunrise or sunset, or when there is a touch of snow on the mountains in the background.

After turning onto highway 261, Diamond Bar Road (signage to Grand Canyon West is extensive so don't worry about getting lost), the road begins a climb into the mountains. Take advantage of the pullouts and scenic viewpoints to get the most out of this trip. It will also provide breaks, so you avoid feeling pushed. On occasion traffic can be quite heavy as Grand Canyon West is a popular attraction and a number of companies provide bus tours from Las Vegas, Nevada.

I recommend a stop at Grand Canyon Western Ranch. This historic ranch that dates to the days when this was the frontier in the Arizona Territory is now a fun little resort. Helicopter tours over the canyon are offered. Camping options run from fancy glamping tents to rustic cabins. There are trail rides on horseback or by horse drawn wagon, buffalo for photo ops, cowboy entertainment at night around the fire,and an authentic western styled restaurant.

The restaurant was once the home of Tap Duncan who established the Diamond Bar Ranch shortly after arriving in the Arizona Territory. Duncan, originally from Texas, had been working in Idaho when he tangled with outlaws that rode with Butch Cassidy and the Sundance Kid. That incident served as incentive for relocation to Arizona. There are a couple of interesting historic footnotes associated with Duncan and the ranch.

When outlaw Kid Curry was killed in Parachute, Colorado, after a train robbery, it was reported that Tap Duncan had been killed. Curry and Duncan's family had been neighbors in Texas, and Curry had been living in Colorado under an alias.

In 1925, Buster Keaton, the comedian and film producer, came to Kingman in search of a suitable location for filming a new movie, *Go West*. The Hollywood celebrity made the Hotel Beale his headquarters. According to local legend, Duncan kept a room at the hotel for use on his occasional trips to Kingman. The rest as they say is history. Duncan met Keaton at the hotel saloon, and the Diamond Bar Ranch was transformed into a set for Keaton's new picture.

After climbing through a narrow, scenic canyon, the highway tops out on a plateau that stretches to the canyon. Please note, near the head of the canyon you will be entering the Hualapai Reservation. It is signed accordingly. Leaving the road is not allowed without a permit.

The one-of-a-kind Grand Canyon West resort is built on the site of what was once a very unusual mining operation. Shortly after WWII, a bat guano mining operation in a cave on the north side of the river commenced. The guano with its high nitrate content was a valuable fertilizer. Initially it was mined,

lowered to the river, shipped by barge to Pierce Ferry and trucked into Kingman.

Freiday Construction in Kingman took it to a new level with construction of a cable car system across the Grand Canyon. It was an engineering marvel. As it turned out the deposits were not as expansive as estimated, the operation closed, and the mining company went bust. The cable remained strung across the canyon until being clipped by an Air Force jet on a training maneuver.

Vestiges from this odd chapter in mining history are but one of the things that make Grand Canyon West special. Grand Canyon West has amenities not found anywhere else along the Grand Canyon. There is an opportunity to get a bird's eye view of the Colorado River at the bottom of the canyon through the glass deck. There are combination helicopter and boat tours, a white-water rafting tour with Hualapai River Runners, a zip line, and exhibits of Native American history at the Native American Village at scenic Guano Point. The restaurant is perched on the canyon rim, and at Hualapai Ranch, you can rent a cabin and enjoy a stunning starlit night.

On the return trip, retrace your steps to Stockton Hill Road. But rather than turn south toward Kingman, continue on highway 25 to Dolan Springs and U.S. 93. The drive is scenic and pleasant, and stands in stark contrast to U.S. 93, the corridor that connects Phoenix with Las Vegas.

On the return drive to Kingman, watch for highway 125 and the turn off to Chloride, a fascinating old town with colorful street names such as Payroll Avenue. Established in the 1860s. this is the oldest continuously inhabited mining town in Arizona. Now mostly a haven for retirees, there are lots of photo opportunities that hearken to the territorial era. One of these is the old depot for the Arizona & Utah Railroad established in 1899 to connect Chloride with the main line of the Atchison, Topeka & Santa Fe Railway at McConnico. There is even an excellent restaurant, Yesterday's, housed in an old stage station and livery complex.

The drive back into Kingman is scenic but hard to enjoy with the traffic. There is, however, one more surprise. Just as you enter town, the first road on the left is Fort Beale Drive. Follow this about 2 miles to the parking lot at Camp Beale Springs. This is the gateway to the Cerbat Foothills Recreation Area, a

35-mile system of hiking and mountain bike trails that provides access to Monolith Gardens, a natural wonder that has been described as a miniature Monument Valley.

The crown jewel is the desert oasis of Beale Springs, about 100 easy yards from the parking lot. The spring and small stream with raw stone bluffs as a backdrop, and the ruins, make this a rare urban gem.

This was once home to the Cerbat clan of the Hualapai Tribe. Father Garces camped here during his expedition in 1776. Early American explorers also camped here including Lt. Beale who led a camel caravan across northern Arizona as he mapped the Beale Wagon Road in 1857 and 1858. A hostelry was established here in the 1860s to provide a restful haven for travelers on the Mohave Prescott Toll Road that connected Fort Mohave and Hardyville on the Colorado River with Fort Whipple at Prescott. During the Hualapai Wars in the 1870s, the military outpost of Camp Beale was established here. Small kiosks scattered around the springs highlight the location of various buildings.

With the subjugation of the Hualapai people, an internment camp was established at this site before the captives were force marched to a reservation on the Colorado River. In the late nineteenth century, a ranch was established here and then a small resort with swimming pool. An automobile road was cut through the site in 1914. Needless to say, this site is more than a beautiful photo op and respite from the desert heat.

This loop drive is filled with surprises. Plan accordingly and savor the adventure. This is an opportunity to experience the best that Arizona has to offer. I recommend fall, winter, or spring for exploration to beat the heat. However, keep in mind that if you make this a winter adventure, you may encounter snow at the Grand Canyon.

GRAND CANYON WEST HAS AMENITIES NOT FOUND ANYWHERE ELSE ALONG THE GRAND CANYON, INCLUDING HELICOPTER TOURS.

IOANA CATALINA E/SHUTTERSTOCK

Chapter 3

SOUTHERN

CALIFORNIA

By David M. Wyman

IN DELANO, EXIT CALIFORNIA HIGHWAY
99 AND TRAVEL WEST ON CALIFORNIA
HIGHWAY 155 (GARCES HIGHWAY).
TURN RIGHT ONTO CALIFORNIA
HIGHWAY 43 FOR THE 5-MILE DRIVE
TO ALLENSWORTH.

San Joaquin Valley's
FREEDOM ROADS

DELANO TO ALLENSWORTH

THIS IS THE COLONEL ALLEN ALLENSWORTH HOME
IN THE STATE PARK BEARING HIS NAME, IN THE
HEART OF THE SAN JOAQUIN VALLEY.

A few pleasant back roads connect Delano, the quintessential San Joaquin Valley town, with Allensworth, which was once the most unique town in the valley. Different as they are, both towns have served as stopping points along the sometimes-arduous roads to freedom.

Delano, at the crossroads of the Garces Highway (State Route 155) and Highway 99 (State Route 99), has long billed itself as "Table Grape Capital of the World." Viewed from Highway 99, Delano appears to be nothing more than a collection of gas stations and fast food restaurants. But Delano also has a vibrant downtown of quaint storefronts. The town looks much the way it did in 1954, when Highway 99 moved from what is now High Street to the new freeway, just to the west and across the railroad tracks.

The Southern Pacific Railroad named the town in 1873 for Columbus Delano, a distant relative of future president Franklin Delano Roosevelt. Delano, who had helped the railroad secure land in the San Joaquin Valley, is not remembered well by history. He served as Secretary of the Interior under the scandal-ridden presidency of Ulysses S. Grant and convinced Grant to veto a bill that would have protected American bison from extermination.

Many citizens of the San Joaquin Valley trace their heritage to Europe. Delano was settled by a large contingent of Yugoslavian immigrants who labored in the vineyards, as well as by Mexican and Chinese railroad workers. A large influx of Latinos began to settle in the San Joaquin Valley in the mid-twentieth century. One of them was César Chavez, a Delano farm worker who would become a seminal figure of the American labor movement in the latter half of the twentieth century. Chavez knew the life of a farm worker in California was not an easy one. He and his family had worked in vineyards up and down the San Joaquin Valley. Chavez, who attended 30 elementary schools, settled in Delano as an adult, where he married a local.

Chavez founded the National Farm Workers Association (NFWA) and worked to win contracts with growers for better pay and benefits for union members. In 1965 the NFWA joined in what became known as the Delano Grape Strike. The farm workers prevailed after a five-year struggle, which included a worldwide boycott of California grapes.

Part of that struggle took place in the vineyards along the Garces Highway, west of Delano, where the farm workers have their Delano union headquarters. The union hall and a few other buildings stand on the north side of the old highway, on a plot of land known as Forty Acres. Here Chavez would meet hold historic meetings with labor leader Walter Reuther and with Robert Kennedy.

Beyond the union hall, the Garces Highway passes by vineyards, orchards, and pasturelands. The highway ends about 5 miles (8 km) west of Delano, at Highway 43 (State Route 43), an alternate north and south route through much of the San Joaquin Valley.

A right turn onto Highway 43 travels north for just over 5 miles, past more farmlands. A left turn onto Palmer leads over an embankment topped with a set of train tracks yhat lead directly into Allensworth State Historic Park.

The park is the site of the first and only community in California founded, constructed, and governed by African Americans. The community was named for Colonel Allen Allensworth, a significant yet largely forgotten figure of American history. Allensworth, born in 1842 in Louisville, Kentucky, grew into adulthood as a slave. Although the education of slaves was illegal, Allensworth learned to read and write. He escaped slavery twice and was captured twice. He won freedom when he escaped a third time during the Civil War. At first he found work as a civilian aide for the Union Army. Later, he joined the Navy and ended the war serving as a first-class petty officer on a gunboat.

After Allensworth underwent a religious conversion, he successfully lobbied for a commission to serve in the all-black 24th Army Infantry as its chaplain. He retired in 1906 as the highest ranking chaplain and the highest-ranking African American in the U.S. Army.

Allensworth moved to Los Angeles where he met William Payne, a black educator. The two men wanted to improve the economic and social status of African Americans. They decided to found an all-black colony and purchased almost nine hundred acres of fertile land in the San Joaquin Valley. By 1910 the colony, with Allensworth's name as the draw, built a town, with an elementary school, a drug store, hotel, stores, churches, and restaurants.

Colonel Allensworth died in 1914, struck by a motorcycle; some believe he was murdered. Without its leader, and facing prejudice from surrounding communities, the town began a slow and seemingly irreversible fade, until the center of Allensworth was completely abandoned in 1966.

Allensworth and the town he founded weren't forgotten. Allensworth State Historical Park was created in 1976. A few of the original buildings still stand, and a few more have been painstakingly reconstructed. The only permanent residents are rangers, who guard the park and guide visitors into the impressive school building, but visitors can stay in a small, tree-shaded campground attached to the park.

While Allensworth State Historical Park showcases what once was and speculates on what might have been, it would be wrong to think that the community was a failure. That's because Allensworth as a community still exists. County Road 84, at the entrance to the state park, connects the old town site with a few hundred homes, many with small plots of land, that stretch out over the flat countryside. County Road 24, off Highway 43, in an alternate route into the community.

Allensworth also has a meeting hall and a school. Most of the residents are Latinos, but there are a few African American residents whose roots extend back to the earlier days of the twentieth century.

After visiting the park and the community, it's easy enough to return to Highway 99 via the Garces Highway, or to make a more leisurely journey along Highway 43 through the vineyards, orchards, and pasturelands of the San Joaquin Valley.

TWO CULTURES BLEND
IN DELANO.

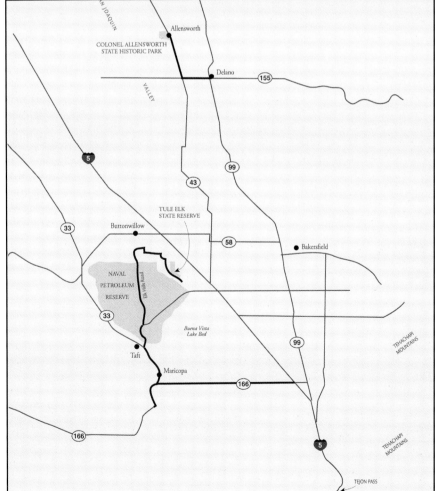

A VINEYARD GROWS ALONG THE GARCES HIGHWAY
(HIGHWAY 155) OUTSIDE OF DELANO.

By David M. Wyman

SOUTHERN MOUNTAINS and DESERTS

THE LAGUNA MOUNTAINS

ORANGE TREES ARE IN BLOSSOM AT THE BASE OF NATE HARRISON GRADE, WHICH SERVES AS AN ALTERNATE, THOUGH RARELY USED, ROUTE FROM THE PAUMA VALLEY TO PALOMAR MOUNTAIN STATE PARK.

START IN TEMECULA, OFF INTERSTATE 15. JUST SOUTH OF OLD TOWN TEMECULA, TURN SOUTH ONTO PALA-TEMECULA ROAD (COUNTY ROAD S16). DRIVE SOUTH TO PALA, THEN HEAD EAST ON CALIFORNIA HIGHWAY 76. TWO ROUTES LEAD FROM HIGHWAY 76 TO THE SLOPES OF PALOMAR MOUNTAIN. WHERE THE GRADE OF HIGHWAY 76 LEVELS OFF, YOU CAN TURN LEFT ONTO COUNTY ROAD S6 (SOUTH GRADE ROAD). OR YOU CAN TURN LEFT ONTO NATE HARRISON GRADE AND GO NORTH. NATE HARRISON GRADE, WHICH BECOMES A WELL-GRADED DIRT ROAD, ENDS AT COUNTY ROAD S6, WHERE A LEFT TURN WILL TAKE YOU FARTHER UPCOUNTRY. FROM THE MOUNT PALOMAR OBSERVATORY, RETRACE YOUR ROUTE TO HIGHWAY 76 AND FOLLOW IT EAST TO ITS JUNCTION WITH HIGHWAY 79. TURN RIGHT ONTO HIGHWAY 79 SOUTH TO REACH JULIAN.

THE PALA MISSION, INCLUDING ITS BELL TOWER, LOOKS MUCH AS IT DID WHEN IT WAS CONSTRUCTED BY THE SPANISH IN 1816.

The Laguna Mountains, rising out of the backcountry of San Diego County, are rich both in beauty and history. These mountains can easily be explored along Highways 76 and 79 (State Routes 76 and 79) and a few adjacent back roads.

A good place to start is Old Town Temecula, with its Old West storefronts that house antique stores and restaurants. At one time the old storefronts were all there in Temecula, but after World War Two the rural landscape around the town began to give way to suburbia. Now Temecula, just off the Interstate 15, is a bedroom community for San Diego to the south. Housing developments are chewing up the rural landscape. But Old Town Temecula still displays quaint charm.

From Temecula, Highway 79 travels south along Temecula Creek. Until the early 1990s, the landscape here was largely rural, but today the first few miles along Highway 79 run through a gauntlet of residential and commercial developments. The rural character of the land returns once the highway begins to climb out of the Temecula Valley and into the Laguna foothills. Highway 79 heads towards historic Warner Springs and Anza-Borrego State Park, which is

on the far side of the mountains.

Just east of Temecula, S16 (County Road S16) travels south to the community of Pala. Today Pala, at the intersection of S16 and Highway 76, is an Indian reservation. Long ago it was the site of a Native American village nestled in the oak and scrub brush foothills at the base of the mountains, where Pala Creek enters the San Luis Rey River. The villagers called themselves the Payomkawichum, people of the west. The Spanish called them the Luiseño, after the San Luis Rey Mission built by the Spanish, about 25 miles to the west.

The Catholic Church built the Pala Mission as a sub-mission to the San Luis Rey Mission in 1816. The Pala Mission still stands, looking much as it did in the early nineteenth century. The chapel walls are decorated with original native designs; massive beams hold up the roof. The mission has a quiet courtyard and the cemetery lies outside the thick chapel walls. The bell tower is unique among the missions of California, for it stands separately from the main building. The mission is different in another way: it alone continues to focus on serving the sizeable Native American community, while all the other missions

in California dating to the Spanish era have turned into museums or serve as ordinary churches.

Today, there are a few additions to the mission, including a gift shop and a museum of gemology (a mining operation for tourmaline, a semi-precious stone, is nearby). The little Pala Market sits across the road from the mission. Part grocery store, part deli, part post office, it serves as an informal meeting place for many local residents. The tamales alone are reason for a visit.

While the Luiseño Indians still live in and around Pala, they share the land with another tribe, the Cupeño. It was not always so. For untold centuries, the Cupeño had lived in higher country to the east, around an area of hot springs in a place they called Cupa. The Spanish knew it as Agua Caliente. Now Cupa is a little resort community known as Warner Springs along Highway 79.

Although the Spanish took ownership of the land away from the Cupeño, the Indians continued to live and work at Cupa for more than a century. In 1892, John G. Downey purchased land at Warner Springs and brought suit to force the Cupeño off the land. Downey had emigrated from Ireland during the gold rush who

THE UPPER PORTION OF THE NATE
HARRISON GRADE PASSES BENEATH A
FOREST OF OAKS AND PINES.

worked as a pharmacist in Los Angeles. He went on to found the city of Downey, east of Los Angeles, and serve as governor of California.

After back and forth battles in state courts, the United States Supreme Court ruled against the Cupeño in 1901. Two years later the Indians were physically evicted from their ancestral home and brought to the Pala Indian reservations.

More than a century after moving to Pala, the Cupeño celebrate their heritage with the Cupa Days festival on the first weekend of May.

Beyond Pala, Highway 76 winds generally southeast up along the course of the San Luis Rey River, through the fertile Pauma Valley. At the head of the valley Highway 76 and the river

MESA GRANDE ROAD, JUST OFF CALIFORNIA
HIGHWAY 79 AND CLOSE TO THE SANTA YSABEL
MISSION, OFFERS A SCENIC ROUTE INTO THE
BACKCOUNTRY OF SAN DIEGO COUNTY.

THE TOWN OF JULIAN IS FAMOUS FOR ITS APPLE PIES. THE
JULIAN PIE COMPANY, MOM'S AND APPLE ALLEY ARE THE
AUTHOR'S FAVORITE BAKERIES.

turn suddenly east, twisting steeply up toward the flanks of Palomar Mountain. Where the grade levels out, S6 (County Road S6) takes off for Palomar Mountain State Park and the famous Palomar Observatory, with its 200-inch telescope.

Nate Harrison Grade, climbing out of the Pauma Valley, offers an alternative route to Palomar Mountain. The mostly dirt road was named for a former slave who took up residence on the mountain. Harrison lived on the mountain for more than 70 years, greeting visitors who passed by his home with buckets of cold spring water. Until a new road was built in the 1940s to haul the telescope up to the observatory, Nate Harrison Grade was the only route up the mountain.

Initially paved, Nate Harrison Grade rises above orange groves, turns to dirt and switchbacks up the mountain, almost to Boucher Point (named for a Basque sheep herder), 5,438 feet above

sea level. On clear days, Catalina Island, 83 miles to the northwest, is visible from the point. Up here the mountain conifers and oaks have created a thick forest.

Nate Harrison Grade continues through beautiful Palomar Mountain State Park. A number of hiking trails lead out from the park, which also includes a campground, picnic areas, and a fishing pond. Beyond the park, Nate Harrison Grade ends at S6, which in turn travels about 7 miles to the top of the mountain and ends at the Mt. Palomar Observatory. A large glass window inside the building gives a view of the massive telescope, one of the largest in the world.

Beyond the junction with S6, Highway 76 follows the course of the San Luis Rey River through a rugged canyon filled with oaks and sycamores. The Highway 76 ends at Highway 79, a few miles past the headwaters of the river, which issue from Lake Henshaw.

A left turn on Highway 79 leads to Warner Springs and Temecula. A right turn, to the south, travels past the old Santa Isabel church. Drivers can head West toward San Diego or south toward the tourist-friendly town of Julian.

Julian began life as a mining camp in 1869, when gold was discovered at nearby Coleman Creek. Although the mines played out, Julian struck it rich as a resort town. The Julian Hotel, one of the original buildings, is one of the oldest continuously operating hotels in southern California. The Eagle and High Peak Mine offers guided tours of its operational gold mine. The cold winters in Julian are ideal for growing apples; the first apple trees in Julian were planted in the early 1870s. Today folks know Julian as much for its abundant crop of gift shops as for its apple pies and ciders and its Old West architecture.

From Julian, roads lead east down into Anza-Borrego State Park and south through the Lagunas toward Interstate 8.

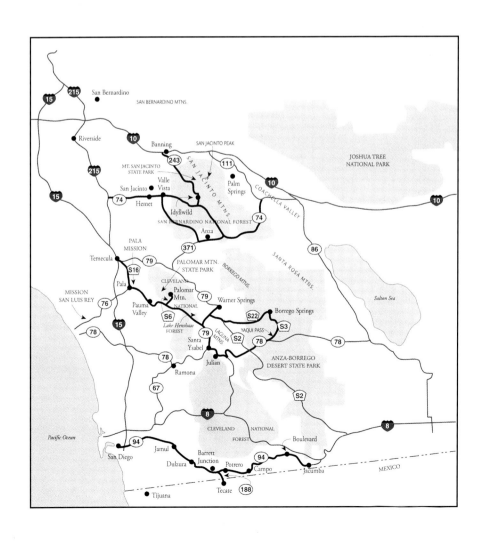

By David M. Wyman

MOJAVE DESERT and HISTORIC ROUTE 66

VICTORVILLE TO AMBOY

A CUSTOMIZED LICENSE PLATE ADORNS THE FRONT OF A 1960 NASH RAMBLER PERMANENTLY PARKED AT THE CLASSIC ROUTE 66 MOTEL. THE MOTEL WAS REPUTEDLY BUILT IN 1929, MAKING IT THE OLDEST MOTOR COURT MOTEL IN THE TOWN OF BARSTOW.

THE LEGENDARY BOTTLE TREE RANCH BETWEEN VICTORVILLE AND BARSTOW IS WORTH A STOP.

FROM INTERSTATE 15 AT VICTORVILLE, TAKE THE PALMDALE ROAD EXIT AND FOLLOW THE ROUTE 66 SIGNS ALONG 7TH STREET TO D STREET. TURN LEFT AND FOLLOW SIGNS ONTO THE NATIONAL TRAILS HIGHWAY, WHICH IS ALSO SIGNED AS ROUTE 66. THE HIGHWAY RUNS NORTH THROUGH ORO GRANDE AND THEN TURNS EAST TOWARD BARSTOW. FROM BARSTOW, FOLLOW INTERSTATE 40 EAST, THEN REGAIN ROUTE 66 A FEW MILES LATER AS A FRONTAGE ROAD. DRIVE 20 MILES TO NEWBERRY SPRINGS. TO REACH THE PISGAH CRATER, FOLLOW THE FRONTAGE ROAD ANOTHER 10 MILES EAST, THEN TURN RIGHT ONTO HECTOR ROAD. BACK ON THE FRONTAGE ROAD, CONTINUE 10 MILES EAST TO LUDLOW. FROM HERE, LEAVE INTERSTATE 40 AND FOLLOW ROUTE 66 TO AMBOY.

Some of the Mojave Desert landscape along famed Route 66 is spectacular. But scenery it is not the primary reason for exploring the old highway. The road itself and the colorful cultural debris along it are the real draws.

Long ago Route 66 was not a back road. It was "The Mother Road" and "America's Main Street." Created by an act of Congress in 1926, Route 66 connected a series of roads that led for 2,448 miles from Chicago to Los Angeles. The road led successive waves of travelers west. Among

them were Dust Bowl refugees of the Great Depression whom author John Steinbeck wrote about in his famous book, *The Grapes of Wrath*. Next came World War II veterans and their families. In 1946, Bobby Troup wrote "Route 66" which became the highway's theme song after Nat King Cole recorded it that same year. It was precisely when tourists, who formed the last great wave of travelers, began to get their kicks on Route 66.

The highway ended its unbroken run in 1985, when the I-40 was completed and the last stretch of the old highway

was decommissioned. Now it exists as a series of segmented back roads. Even so, interest in Route 66 has never faded. Evoking a powerful sense of nostalgia, new "Historic Route 66" highway signs have sprouted along much of the old road and colorful neon still lights the way to old motor courts and diners. But much of the glory of Route 66 has faded.

In California, Route 66 cruises for 320 miles between the Colorado River, near the town of Needles, and the Santa Monica Pier, at the Pacific Ocean. During the heyday of Route 66, most travelers drove from east to west. But our tour reverses the direction, traveling from the town of Victorville to the community at Amboy.

The starting point is the Palm Avenue exit off the Interstate 15 in Victorville. Named for a Santa Fe Railroad superintendent in 1885, Victorville is a medium sized but fast growing town 85 miles east of Los Angeles. The highway follows its original path along Seventh Street in Old Town Victorville, to D Street, where the heritage of the highway is still celebrated at the California Route 66 Museum.

Crossing under the I-15, D Street continues both as Route 66 and as the National Trails Highway. The Iron

A SERVICE STATION IN NEWBERRY SPRINGS NO LONGER HAS GASOLINE TO SELL. JUDGING FROM THE PRICE ON THE PUMP, THE STATION HAS BEEN CLOSED A LONG TIME.

A VISITOR TO THE PISGAH CRATER

EXITS A LAVA TUBE.

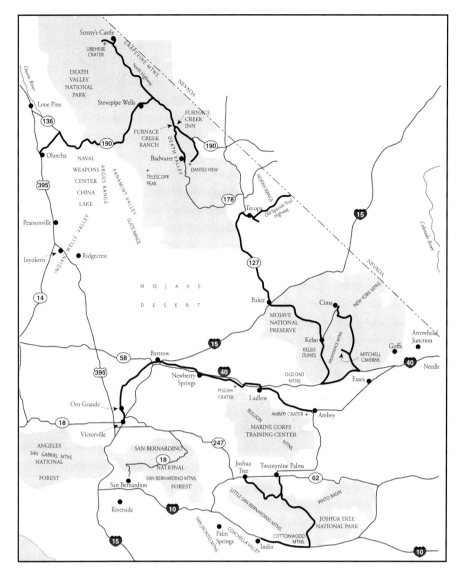

DODGE CORONET TAILFINS IN BARSTOW.

Hog restaurant and saloon and a few gift shops await visitors in the little community of Oro Grande. Beyond Victorville, the highway continues north through the community of Oro Grande and along the usually dry Mojave River, where massive cement factories have replaced the failed dreams of nineteenth-century gold miners. The San Gabriel Mountains, snowcapped in winter, serve as a backdrop in the west.

Route 66 turns east and passes by the ruins of old stores, a post office, service stations, and auto courts. Watch for the "Bottle Tree Ranch" on the west side of the highway, where hundreds of colorful old bottles hang on scores of poles that look like tall hat racks.

The views across the desert are expansive as Route 66 reaches Main Street where it enters the city of Barstow. An important junction since prehistoric times, first for Naive Americans, then the Spanish and American pioneers, Barstow today is the western terminus for the I-40. Barstow also serves as the eastern end for State Highway 58, which travels west toward the San Joaquin Valley. The I-15 continues east into Nevada and is the major weekend route for Californians headed to Las Vegas.

Like Victorville, Barstow was named for a railroad superintendent, and it's home to the enormous BNSF railyard. Casa Desierto, one of the "Harvey Houses" established as dining rooms and boarding houses along the Santa Fe Railroad line, was built in 1911; it is a couple blocks off Main Street. Long abandoned, Casa Desierto was renovated in the 1990s, and now is home to the Amtrak station, the Mother Road Route 66 Museum, and the Western America Railroad Museum.

Main Street leads past a cornucopia of fast food restaurants, gas stations, and motels. The Route 66 Motel, one of the town's original motor courts, boasts a spectacular neon sign and has a collection of old cars and other Route 66 artifacts. Beyond the town, Route 66 is temporarily submerged by the I-40, to resurface a few miles later as a rough frontage road. Desert mountains now closely flank the south side of the road. About 20 miles past Barstow, the frontage road veers north into the little community of Newberry Springs. The Bagdad Cafe, where the 1984 cult movie of the same name was filmed, draws visitors from around the world. The food is delicious and some of the locals, who enjoyed playing bit parts in the film, frequent the café.

The Pisgah Crater, a cinder cone estimated to have erupted sometime less than 100,000 years ago, is about 10 miles east of Newberry Springs. It can be reached by taking the exit for Hector Road, off either the I-40 or the Route 66 frontage road. Some of the cone has been removed to make roadbeds for train tracks, but active mining seems to have stopped. It's possible to drive a passenger car almost to the top of the cone, and the short walk to the summit offers a spectacular 360-degree view of the surrounding desert. Explore the east side of the crater to find numerous lava tubes, some which are several yards in length and large enough to stand up in. Other tubes are just large enough to wriggle through.

About 10 miles past Pisgah, Route 66 takes its leave of the I-40 at the little community of Ludlow. There are a couple of gas stations, a cafe, a pleasant motel, and some deserted building in Ludlow. The next reliable services are about 80 miles east; it's a good idea to top off the gas tank.

A vast open desert valley now runs between the Bullion Mountains to the south, and the Old Dad Mountains to the north. The road parallels the BNSF railroad tracks. After 30 miles, the Amboy Crater, another cinder cone, comes into view. A rough road leads to the base of cone and a short but steep trail travels to the summit.

The tiny community of Amboy is about 10 miles beyond the cinder cone. At one time Amboy was a major rest stop along Route 66. Today only Roy's

Motel and Café, which opened in 1937, remains to provide sporadic services to visitors, with a gas station, a few motel units, and a 50s-style diner.

A few miles south of town, on Amboy Road, the National Chloride Company mines salt for industrial uses. Look for the huge trench gouged into the salt flats, just south of the entry gate to the salt works, on the opposite side of the road.

Amboy is a fitting place to end our Route 66 tour, although there are several options for further exploration. For example, continuing along Route 66 another 32 miles east leads past more ruined outposts of civilization, as well as through the miniscule communities of Essex, Goffs, and Searchlight Junction, before rejoining the I-15 near the California-Arizona border.

Amboy Road heads south for 50 miles through the sparsely populated Wonder Valley until it reaches the town of Twentynine Palms, next to Joshua Tree National Park. Kelbaker Road, a few miles east of Amboy, leads straight back to the I-15. There's even time enough to make the drive back to Barstow to spend a night at the Route 66 Motel.

In the late 1950s, Roy's received a towering new sign and a new building that housed the motel lobby. These modern looking structures were examples of Southern California's classic Astro – or Googie – architecture, which attempted to mimic the technological designs of the then new space age. It is ironic that the dreams for a brighter tomorrow along Route 66 have been detoured to an uncertain future.

LATE-AFTERNOON SUN SHINES ON ROY'S MOTEL AND CAFE AFTER A BRIEF WINTER RAINSTORM.

A COLLECTION OF CLASSIC GAS STATION SIGNS ON HIGHWAY 58 IN BARSTOW.

VINTAGE NEON ON ROUTE 66 IN BARSTOW.

A TRUCK HAS BEEN MIRED IN THE MUD AT THE NATIONAL CHLORIDE COMPANY'S "BONE YARD" SINCE THE MID-TWENTIETH CENTURY.

By Karen Misuraca and Gary Crabbe

THIS SAILBOAT IS ONE OF MANY
ANCHORED IN FRONT OF THE DANA
POINT YACHT CLUB.

DANA'S PILGRIM
and the SWALLOWS
OF SAN JUAN
CAPISTRANO

DANA POINT TO CASPERS WILDERNESS PARK

FROM STATE ROUTE 1 (HIGHWAY 1) WEST OF DANA POINT, TAKE GOLDEN LANTERN STREET SOUTH TO DANA POINT HARBOR DRIVE. FOLLOW DANA POINT HARBOR DRIVE, AND AFTER TAKING IN THE VIEW FROM THE HEADLANDS, RETURN TO HIGHWAY 1 BY GOING NORTH ON GREEN LANTERN STREET. CONTINUE NORTH ON HIGHWAY 1 TO INTERSTATE 5. FOLLOW INTERSTATE 5 NORTH TO THE SAN JUAN CAPISTRANO EXIT, WHERE YOU'LL HEAD INTO THE CITY. FROM SAN JUAN CAPISTRANO, DRIVE 7.5 MILES ON THE ORTEGA HIGHWAY (CALIFORNIA HIGHWAY 74) TO CASPERS WILDERNESS PARK.

Richard Henry Dana Jr.—author of the classic *Two Years Before the Mast,* a rousing narrative about his voyage aboard a square-rigger in 1834—loved the view from the headlands that overlook today's Dana Point Harbor. He often stood on the clifftop at the end of what is now the Street of the Blue Lantern to gaze down at his ship, *The Pilgrim,* on which he served as a sailor on a 150-day voyage from Boston, around Cape Horn, to California.

Describing the coastline, Dana wrote, " . . . It was a beautiful day, and so warm that we had on straw hats, duck trowsers, and all the summer gear; and as this was mid-winter, it spoke well for the climate; and we afterwards found that the thermometer never fell to the freezing point throughout the winter, and that there was very little difference between the seasons . . ."

Many streets in the town of Dana Point are named for the brightly colored glass in *The Pilgrim*'s lanterns, and some streetlights were modeled after maritime signal lanterns. Between Amber Lantern and Violet Lantern streets, with a loop around El Camino Capistrano, visitors and residents stroll on Bluff Top Trail, enjoying the salt air, the harbor views,

and the neighborhood of Cape Cod–style cottages and lovely gardens. At the end of Golden Lantern Street, the sweeping lawns and picnic tables at Lantern Bay Park are pleasant places from which to enjoy the sea breezes.

A replica of Richard Henry Dana's 130-foot ship—a "snow brig" hosting fourteen sails—and a couple thousand modern pleasure craft are berthed in the harbor within a mile-long jetty. Students at the Ocean Institute, a marine science teaching center, live as 1830-era sailors on the ship and also on the *Spirit of Dana Point,* a 118-foot topsail schooner also moored here. The ships, the facility, and the adjacent tide pools are open to the public on Sunday afternoons.

The annual Tall Ships Festival in September, the largest annual gathering of tall ships on the West Coast, is a breathtaking sight from the bluff. During the festival, multimasted brigantines, square topsail schooners, and more historic vessels glide into the harbor in full sail, cannons blasting.

The deck of one of the many waterfront restaurants and Dana Point Harbor Drive that skirts the harbor are vantage points from which to watch a lively parade of watercraft—from kayaks to jet skis and outrigger canoes, fishing

A TOUR DOCENT IN PERIOD DRESS STANDS ABOARD A FULL-SIZE REPLICA OF THE PILGRIM, A TALL SHIP DOCKED AT DANA POINT HARBOR AND BASED ON THE SHIP IMMORTALIZED IN RICHARD HENRY DANA JR.'S CLASSIC NOVEL, *TWO YEARS BEFORE THE MAST*.

The seventh in California's twenty-one mission chain, Mission San Juan today consists of the rustic ruins of the Great Stone Church. The church was established in 1776, completed in 1806, and destroyed by an earthquake in 1812, along with Padre Serra's chapel. Adobe chapel walls surround an impressive, twenty-two-foot-tall, gold-leafed Baroque altarpiece decorated with more than fifty angels. It was carved in Spain three centuries ago and sent to California in 1906. Visitors wander acres of walled gardens and grounds, encountering fountains and exhibits presenting early mission life.

Across the street from the mission, the public library is a striking Morris Graves–designed, postmodern edifice that pays homage to Spanish heritage by the use of stucco walls, mission clay roof tiles, wooden beams, mini-towers, small punched windows, stencil ornamentation, and loggias around a central courtyard.

San Juan Capistrano is also famous for a springtime influx of thousands of swallows. The birds migrate annually to Goya, Argentina, in October and return to their spring and summer home here in March. The Swallows Day Parade and the Fiesta de las Golondrinas celebrate their return. (In recent years, the swallows have shown up in diminishing numbers, yet the festival goes on.)

A walk around the tree-shaded Los Rios Historic District, said to be the oldest residential street in the state, is an introduction to early California architecture. Dozens of adobe homes built for mission families, the earliest dating to 1794, are still in use as residences and restaurants. Famous for hearty breakfasts, the Ramos House Café on Verdugo Street is a board-and-batten house, one of several in the neighborhood erected between the late 1880s and 1910. Next door, the Combs House, now a gift shop called Hummingbird Cottage, was built in 1865 and was moved here in 1878 from an abandoned boomtown.

and whale-watching boats to sailboats and yachts—pass by. Sightseeing cruisers and ferries to Catalina Island are based here, too.

The Pilgrim cruised along the California coast from San Diego to San Francisco in the early 1800s, trading goods for hides from the ranchos and the Spanish missions. Five miles as the crow flies inland from Dana Point, Mission San Juan Capistrano was a major source of cow hides, which were hauled back to Boston for shoemaking. Founded by the Franciscan friar Junipero Serra in 1776, the mission and the leafy streets and historic houses surrounding it invite a pleasant short drive from Dana Point.

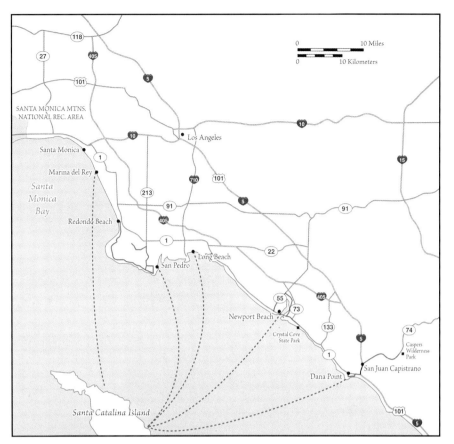

The O'Neill Museum, showcasing local history, resides in a sweet little Victorian home of the late 1870s, while the Mission Revival–style, domed, brick, circa-1894 Santa Fe Railroad station is now a restaurant and Amtrak stop.

Travelers seeking solitude head east on Ortega Highway about 8 miles to Caspers Wilderness Park, a vast array of river terraces and sandstone canyons in the coastal Santa Ana Mountains. Adjacent to the Cleveland National Forest and the Audubon Society's Starr Ranch Sanctuary, the rustic park watered by rocky creeks is mainly groves of coastal live oaks and California sycamores, sage, and chaparral; the landscape here isn't much different from that encountered by the early Spanish explorers. A small museum and a mountain-view terrace at the visitor's center offer a preview of the delights of the park's 30 miles of equestrian and hiking trails.

THE MISSION SAN JUAN CAPISTRANO IS CONSIDERED TO BE THE CROWN JEWEL OF CALIFORNIA MISSIONS. DATING BACK TO ITS ORIGINS OVER TWO HUNDRED YEARS AGO, THE MISSION HAS LONG BEEN A DRAW FOR VISITORS AND STILL CONDUCTS MASS, OFFERS TOURS OF THE OLD STONE BUILDINGS, AND IS THE PLACE THOUSANDS OF SWALLOWS RETURN TO EACH MARCH.

A STATUE OF FATHER SERRA AND A NATIVE AMERICAN BOY STANDS OVER THE MAIN GARDEN AT MISSION SAN JUAN CAPISTRANO. LOCALS OFTEN SEEK OUT THE BEAUTY OF THE MISSION AND ITS GARDENS FOR THEIR ENGAGEMENT, WEDDING, AND ANNIVERSARY PHOTOS.

By Karen Misuraca and Gary Crabbe

The
SEVEN
SISTERS

MORRO BAY AND THE EDNA VALLEY

THE FIRST WARM RAYS OF SUNLIGHT ON MORRO ROCK TURN THE MONOLITH INTO SOMETHING RESEMBLING A HUGE GOLDEN PYRAMID. ON THE WATERFRONT, A PIGEON SITS ALONE ON A WOODEN RAILING, STARING OUT OVER THE CALM BLUE WATERS OF MORRO BAY.

TRANQUIL IS AN UNDERSTATEMENT FOR DESCRIBING THIS SERENE VIEW OF A FULL MOON SETTING AT DAWN OVER A SMALL SAILBOAT ANCHORED IN MORRO BAY.

FROM STATE ROUTE 1 (HIGHWAY 1), TAKE MAIN STREET SOUTH INTO THE TOWN OF MORRO BAY. GO WEST ON MORRO BAY BOULEVARD TO EMBARCADERO ROAD, WHICH SKIRTS THE BAY. DRIVE NORTH TO MORRO ROCK, RETURNING SOUTH ON EMBARCADERO ROAD TO TIDELANDS PARK. RETURN TO MORRO BAY'S MAIN STREET AND PROCEED SOUTH TO MORRO BAY STATE PARK ROAD. FROM THERE, CONTINUE SOUTH TO SOUTH BAY BOULEVARD, WHERE YOU'LL HEAD SOUTH AGAIN. AT LOS OSOS VALLEY ROAD, HEAD WEST TO MONTAÑA DE ORO STATE PARK. THEN TAKE LOS OSOS VALLEY ROAD SOUTHEAST TO CALIFORNIA HIGHWAY 227, WHERE YOU'LL HEAD SOUTH ON THE HIGHWAY INTO THE EDNA VALLEY AND LOOP BACK NORTH ON ORCUTT ROAD TO U.S. HIGHWAY 101 NEAR SAN LUIS OBISPO.

The California version of the Rock of Gibraltar, a craggy, 576-foot-tall peak called Morro Rock looms as a dark sentinel at the mouth of Morro Bay. The seventh in a chain of fifty-million-year-old volcanic plug domes, or morros, called the Seven Sisters, Morro Rock is a sailor's landmark and a nesting site for peregrine falcons. One of a handful of natural coastal estuaries still existing in this country, the bay and surrounding marsh shelter thousands of birds. These include more than two dozen endangered and threatened species,

notably the sand-colored western snowy plover and the least tern. One of the largest overwintering bird sites in North America, the estuary is also an important great blue heron rookery and a nursery for newborn sea creatures, such as rays, sharks, and fish.

A magical day begins in early morning, when mist hovers over the still, mirrorlike bay. Snowy egrets and black-crowned night herons stand motionless in the eel grass and pickleweed marsh, in a primordial scene. Common loons, grebes, and teal float between the dense

MORRO BAY STATE
PARK IS HOME TO THIS
PROTECTED BIRD
ROOKERY, WHERE
HERONS AND
CORMORANTS RETURN
AT SUNSET TO THEIR
NESTS PERCHED HIGH
IN THESE TREES.

grasses, searching for insects. Belted kingfishers—vibrant blue and white with rakish topknots—perch on the reeds, then hover and dive into the shallow waters for small fish. The heads of curious harbor seals, sea lions, and sea otters bob up near fishing boats as they glide out through the narrow bay entrance into the open ocean.

Sightseers and birdwatchers park their vehicles at the foot of Morro Rock, while on the north side of the rock, surfers ride the waves off Morro Strand State Beach. At the south end of Embarcadero Road, the street that skirts the bay, Tidelands Park is another pleasant spot from which to contemplate the bay, have a picnic, or launch a kayak. Canoes and kayaks are the transport of choice here for bird-watchers who find this one of the richest habitats in the state, considering that more than 90 percent of California's coastal wetlands have disappeared due to development.

Headquartered at the Morro Bay State Park Museum of Natural History, the annual Winter Bird Festival attracts about five hundred enthusiasts in January, when a typical false spring bathes Morro Bay and the Central Coast in winter warmth and bird migrations are at their peak.

On the west side of the bay in Montaña de Oro State Park, on narrow beaches protected from the open sea by a 4-mile-long sand spit, you'll find Morro Dunes Natural Preserve. The preserve consists of scrub-covered dunes up to one hundred feet high. Vista points afford lovely coastline views, while footpaths lead to the dunes and the beaches. About 50 miles of hiking, biking, and equestrian trails ramble through the hills and riparian stream canyons above.

Off Los Osos Valley Road, the Los Osos Oaks State Reserve is a ninety-acre grove of eight-hundred-year-old,

SIMILAR TO THOSE SIGNS IN THE NORTHERN CALIFORNIA SISTER VALLEYS OF NAPA AND SONOMA, GUIDE WINE LOVERS IN THE EDNA VALLEY WITH HELPFUL ARROWS THAT POINT THE WAY TO VARIOUS WINERIES ALONG THE SAN LUIS OBISPO COASTAL WINE TRAIL.

dwarfed, mossy, gnarled coast live oaks on ancient dunes. Drivers on this road can see the other six morros, all in a row, parading east into the winelands of the Edna Valley.

Just 4 miles from the ocean, homesteading pioneers planted the first grape vines in the Edna Valley, along with apple orchards and grain crops, in the late 1870s. Some of those Zinfandel vineyards continue to produce today, thriving in the sea breezes that funnel through the 4-mile-wide valley and lower the summer temperatures, allowing a long season for the grapes to develop the intense, complex flavors of the famous Edna Valley chardonnays, pinot noirs, syrahs, and white rhone varietals.

California Highway 227 rolls through the valley below the low foothills of the Santa Lucia Mountains past vineyards, old farms and orchards, and signs advertising "Hay for Sale." A dozen or so premium wineries are scattered throughout the valley, alongside horse and cattle ranches. The best view of the Edna Valley and the Seven Sisters morros is from the terrace of Edna Valley Vineyard, one of the oldest wineries in the state. It's famous for its chardonnay, some of which comes from decades-old vines.

Just up the road at Old Price Canyon Road and Highway 227, the Old Edna Townsite is a welcome stop for deli lunches and wine tasting. This is the site where in the early 1880s stagecoaches

stopped regularly, and dairy and cattle farmers in the valley patronized the livery stables, the large creamery, and the slaughterhouse. At the time, the township of Edna was also home to a hotel, a railroad depot, and three saloons—one for the cattlemen, one for the Pacific Coast Railroad workers, and one for asphalt miners. In 1906, Edna had a population of nearly two thousand when a local dairyman built a mercantile and dance hall large enough for one hundred couples. By the 1930s, valley residents were automobile owners and drove into San Luis Obispo for their needs, so the town of Edna waned. Eventually, all of the buildings except a barn, the railroad depot, and Edna Hall—and today's store—either burned down or crumbled.

ROWS OF YOUNG WINE GRAPE VINES STRETCH
OUT ALONG THE GREEN HILLS OF SAN LUIS OBISPO
COUNTY'S EDNA VALLEY IN SPRING, GIVING PROMISE
TO THE COMING HARVEST.

On a short detour on Corbett Canyon Road, a vintage tractor on the roadside marks the tasting room at Kynsi Winery, housed in a restored 1940s dairy. On the Talley Vineyards estate stands a two-story, restored adobe home built in 1863 on the Mexican land grant, Rancho Santa Manuela. Wine lovers stop in to taste Talley chardonnay, which has been described as redolent of peaches, apricots, citrus, and hazelnut oil. Biddle Regional Park invites a stroll or a picnic beneath huge old sycamores and oaks.

Toward the north end of Orcutt Road, in a circa-1909, bright yellow former schoolhouse, Baileyana Winery offers tastes of a ruby-colored, berry-flavored pinot noir. Valley views are stunning from here, and visitors are welcome to linger for a game of croquet or bocce ball.

A HORSEBACK RIDER SITS ATOP HER HORSE AFTER RIDING THROUGH THE SAND DUNES AND BEACHES BETWEEN THE OCEAN AND MORRO BAY AT MONTAÑA DE ORO STATE PARK.

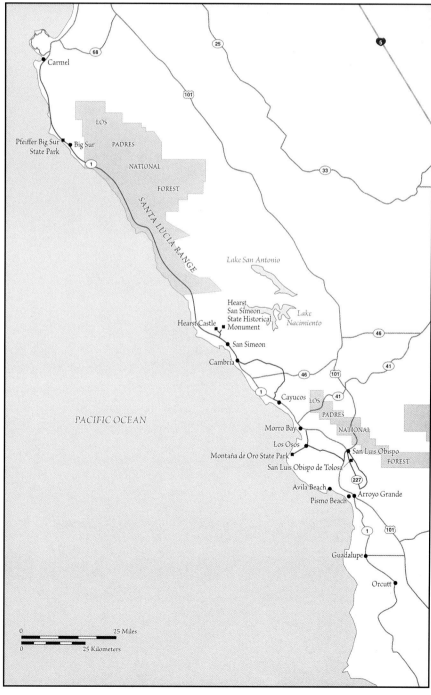

Chapter 4

NORTHERN
CALIFORNIA

By David M. Wyman

PAST THE CITY OF STOCKTON, TAKE CALIFORNIA STATE ROUTE 12 OFF OF U.S. INTERSTATE 5 AND TRAVEL WEST. AFTER REACHING ANDRUS ISLAND, TURN RIGHT OFF OF HIGHWAY 12 ONTO TERMINOUS ROAD AND CONTINUE TO THE TOWN OF ISLETON. TURN LEFT ONTO STATE ROUTE 160. CONTINUE THROUGH THE TOWN OF WALNUT GROVE TO LOCKE.

Where it's ALWAYS YESTERDAY

LOCKE AND THE DELTA

PART OF THE ONE-BLOCK-LONG MAIN STREET, LOCKE.

The town of Locke is only about a mile north of Walnut Grove. It was designed by Chinese architects and completed in 1920. It was originally named Lockeport for George Locke, the owner of the land on which the buildings stand, the name of the town was shortened to Locke.

Actually, the first building on the site of Locke went up in 1912, when businessman Chan Tin-San built a saloon on the Locke property. Tin-San apparently understood the business potential of a Southern Pacific Railroad wharf and warehouse located across the levee.

In the 1940s, farm workers and residents had a choice of restaurants, herb shops, grocery stores, fish markets, and boarding houses. Outsiders could rub elbows with the locals in gambling halls and bordellos. Today, Locke is long past its heyday. And that is precisely why Locke exudes so much unforced, authentically nostalgic charm. In 1970, the town was placed on the National Register of Historic Places.

My travel companion Kathy and I left Walnut Grove and traveled the 1 mile to Locke. We drove slowly past buildings whose second stories rise above the levee and Highway 160; here and there rickety wooden steps led down between the buildings to Main Street, at the base of the levee. Across the highway we could see that Chan Tin-San was right about the old Southern Pacific warehouse, which over the years grew to be more than eight hundred feet long. More than a half dozen fruit packers rented space in the building, but today the warehouse is used to store and launch pleasure boats.

There isn't a lot of parking space in Locke, either alongside Highway 160, or along the one block of Main Street. It's easier to find parking on the north side of town, near the Locke school that now serves as an annex of the Dai Loy Museum, which is at the south end of town.

We strolled along the wooden boardwalks on Main Street. The paint on the storefronts has faded or peeled away,

A BOAT RESTS AT ANCHOR IN THE LOST SLOUGH, INVISIBLE BEHIND A LEVEE FROM NEARBY LOCKE.

MAIN STREET IN LOCKE, CALIFORNIA.

THE SUN SETS BEHIND THE ISLETON BRIDGE.

RYDE HOTEL IN WANUT GROVE.

fire is an ever present danger, some of the buildings seem to lean at precarious angles and many of the shops are vacant. Most of the Chinese residents are gone, too. Today people live in apartments on Main Street or in houses on the southern and eastern ends of town.

Locke, moribund though it may appear, is still very much alive, with several shops, a grocery store, and the museum. And there's Al's Place, a bar and restaurant where patrons dine on the local specialties, steak or chicken with peanut butter. Al's also has an unusual mural on the wall behind the bar, picturing Asian cowboys herding cattle.

Kathy and I had Al's sandwiches for lunch. There were more people sitting inside Al's than anywhere else in town. Kathy declined to spread peanut butter on her chicken sandwich. I was more adventurous. Along with peanut butter, I added a healthy amount of apricot jelly to my steak sandwich.

After lunch we wandered through the Dai Loy Museum, once a bustling gambling house and now the official repository for all things historic in Locke, including Chinese gambling paraphernalia. After visiting the museum we walked behind Main Street. Making our way past houses and little gardens, we wandered no more than a few hundred yards to the base of another levee topped with trees. Scrambling up an almost indistinct trail, we viewed the Lost Slough on the far side of the levee, where pleasure boats sat at anchor in the still waters.

We returned to our car and traveled north again. Beyond Locke, on the east side of the river, we passed some beautifully restored nineteenth-century homes as well as myriad pear orchards. We reached the town of Courtland, home to a pear fair each July, then Hood, perhaps the only town along the river that doesn't have a marina. Clarksburg, settled in 1849, is visible on the west side of the river. The backroad took us away from of the Delta, with the blacktop blending into Freeport Boulevard and continuing on to downtown Sacramento, where the pulse of time began to beat again.

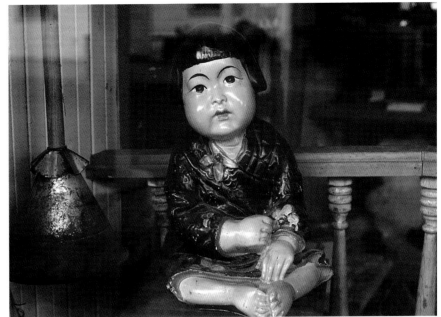

THE KEE SING STORE, WITH THE DAI LOY
MUSEUM IN THE BACKGROUND, SITS ALONG
LOCKE'S MAIN STREET.

A FIGURINE DECORATES A SHOP WINDOW ALONG
MAIN STREET IN LOCKE.

A DOG TAKES A LITTLE REST IN LOCKE.

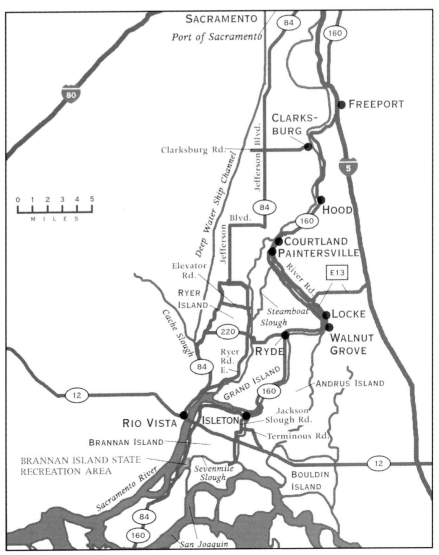

By David M Wyman

The
SACRAMENTO VALLEY

THE MIDWAY

CHINESE PISTACHE TREES, PLANTED BY THE
MEMBERS OF THE DURHAM LADIES CLUB, LINE
THE MIDWAY, THE OLD ROUTE OF HIGHWAY 99.

TAKE CALIFORNIA STATE ROUTE 162 WEST FROM ITS JUNCTION WITH CALIFORNIA STATE ROUTE 99. CONTINUE 3 MILES AND TURN RIGHT ONTO MIDWAY. CONTINUE THROUGH THE TOWN OF DURHAM. MIDWAY TURNS INTO PARK AVENUE IN THE TOWN OF CHICO, PARK AVENUE BECOMES MAIN STREET AND THEN ESPLANDE. CONTINUE ONTO HIGHWAY 99. TRAVEL NORTH FOR ABOUT 13 MILES AND EXIT HIGHWAY 99 ONTO SOUTH AVENUE AT VINA. TURN RIGHT ONTO ROWLES ROAD, THEN LEFT ONTO 7TH STREET AND RIGHT ONTO STEPHENS ROAD TO THE NEW CLAIRVAUX MONASTERY AND VINEYARD.

AUDREY BROCHHEUSER IN 1999 ON THE FRONT PORCH OF HER HOME, THE DURHAM HOUSE (NOW THE DURHAM HOUSE INN).

I hadn't driven along the Midway, a two-lane stretch of road that runs from Richvale to Chico, since 1970. The Midway, reputedly the oldest concrete roadway in California, was once part of Highway 99, the Central Valley's first major roadway. Until the 1960's, when freeway bypasses were constructed, Highway 99 actually ran through the center of several towns.

In the early 1960s, the Highway 99 roadbed moved about a mile east of the Midway, gaining two lanes and becoming a freeway. The Midway, no longer a state highway, was relegated to the simple task of serving local traffic. I had taken the old road a few times when I was a student at California State University, Chico, because I prided myself on exploring every back road around Chico.

I had only vague memories of what the Midway looked like when I made my return trip one recent autumn. The Midway's chief attraction, I knew, was that it would take me off the busy Highway 99 freeway. I had driven north from Sacramento that morning, through 80 miles of rice fields and walnut groves, ultimately on my way to destinations well north of Durham and Chico. About 30 miles north of Sacramento I passed the twin cities of Yuba City and Marysville, separated only by the Sacramento River. To the west I could see the striking Sutter Buttes, reputedly the world's smallest mountain chain. I crossed from Sutter County into Butte County and, still about 19 miles from Chico, reached the junction of Highway 99 and Highway 162.

If I'd turned right, Highway 162 would have taken me east, into the city of Oroville, which sits up against the Sierra Nevada foothills. Instead, I turned left, heading west through a vast expanse of rice fields. Huge rice elevators and silos were visible in the distance. Highway 162, followed far enough west, heads up into the Coast Range. I did drive the first 2 miles along Highway 162, crossing a set of train tracks. Just beyond the tracks I turned right, at the southern end of the Midway. There were more rice fields along both sides of the narrow road. I passed through the little community of Richvale, where the most prominent structures were tall rice silos. Continuing toward Durham, my view east was cut off by the slightly elevated roadbed of the train tracks which now paralleled the Midway. An egret stood on the west of side of the road, its feathers a bright white against the rice grass, colored an autumn brown.

known as the Durham House Inn. The mansion is east of the railroad tracks on the Durham Dayton Highway, and so escaped the conflagration that engulfed the center of town. In 1871 the California and Oregon Railroad laid tracks to a flour mill built by Durham, and "Durham's Stop" soon grew to become the community of Durham.

As I continued my drive north, toward Chico, I marveled at the beautiful trees that lined each side of Midway, trees I couldn't identify. There was a hint of the autumn color to come, with some of the elongated leaves showing pale red and orange. I parked at the Hodge's Nursery and Tree Farm about a quarter of a mile past the four way stop sign in Durham. The owner, Ken Hodge, graciously showed me around his property and told me a little about the trees on the Midway.

They were, Mr. Hodge explained, Chinese pistache trees, Pistacia chinensis, and he confirmed my suspicions that they would be ablaze with color in a few weeks. And they were planted to honor the memory of various members of the Durham Ladies Club. "But the color won't last long," Mr. Hodge told me. "One good storm and the leaves will be gone." I told Mr. Hodge I would call in a few weeks to see if the trees were at their autumn best, so that I could photograph them, and have an excuse to return to the Midway. We said goodbye and I continued to the end of the Midway, crossing over the train tracks on a bridge leading into Chico.

The Midway changed names in Chico, to become Park Avenue and then Main Street, all the route of old Highway 99. Downtown Chico, complete with stoplights, is hardly a byway, but it has managed to keep its small town flavor and is far more fun to drive than the freeway, just to the east.

Shubert's Ice Cream & Candy shop has been in operation since 1938, and doesn't seem to face any stiff competition. If you have a dog, the owners, Nate Pulliam and Kasey Pulliam-Reynolds, fourth generation owners, or their children, might treat your pet to some ice cream, too.

About 10 miles past Richvale I arrived at the community of Durham. At the intersection of the Midway and the Durham Dayton-Highway, which makes up the commercial district in town, I had a good cup of coffee at the French Bakery, across the road from the town's country store. Since my visit, the bakery has morphed into the excellent Pueblito Mexican Grill.

Durham can boast no buildings from the Gold Rush era, for none of them survived a 1938 fire. The town, though, can boast about the beautiful Durham House, a restored Victorian mansion, built in 1874 by William Durham for his bride, Minnie, and now

KENDALL HALL, BUILT OF BRICK IN 1929 IN
THE ROMANESQUE STYLE, REFLECTS THE LATE
AFTERNOON LIGHT OF THE DAY AT CHICO STATE.

But I noted one change from my own days in Chico: there are several bike shops. That wasn't a surprise, because Chico has been voted the most bike friendly town in the nation. On a whim, I decided to stop at Pullins Cyclery, one of the bike shops in town when I lived in Chico. I'd chatted a few times with old Mr. Pullin, whose shop was cluttered with old bike parts. The current owner, Steve O'Bryan, worked for Mr. Pullin as a high school student at the same time I was a student at Chico State.

Mr. O'Bryan enjoys repairing old bikes and telling a good story, thereby keeping alive two traditions that were long associated with his mentor. His shop boasted many of the most technologically sophisticated mountain bikes, but he was more proud of a restored Schwinn "Deluxe Tornado."

After saying goodbye to Mr. O'Bryan, I continued up Main Street, which becomes the Esplanade at the north end of downtown. Like the Midway, the Esplanade was lined with trees, though not the Chinese pistache. Instead, there were elms, flaming ambers, and, along the center divider, ginkgo trees. Unlike the rural Midway, Esplanade is also lined by a number of lovely homes, some dating from the last century.

The beautiful Cal State Chico campus sits just west of the Esplanade. So does the Bidwell Mansion, which was built by the town's founder, John Bidwell, and features a pink tinted stucco exterior.

Construction began in 1865 and lasted three years. Bidwell apparently wanted the mansion, which has twenty six rooms, to look like an Italian villa. The college eventually took control of the mansion after the death of Bidwell's

A STONE BENCH BENEATH AN OAK TREE
INVITES A MEDITATIVE MOMENT AT THE ABBEY
OF NEW CLAIRVAUX IN VINA.

THE ABBEY CHURCH AT THE NEW CLAIRVAUX
MONASTERY IN THE COMMUNITY OF VINA.

widow, Annie, using it at various times as a girls' dormitory, a dining hall, classrooms, and college dances. In 1964 California turned the mansion into a state historic park.

After visiting the mansion, I walked across a footbridge spanning Big Chico Creek, which spills out of the mountains and makes its way through the Chico State campus. I'd forgotten just how pretty the campus is. Originally built on eight acres of a cherry orchard set aside by the Bidwells, the college was originally named the Northern Branch of the State Normal School.

Leaving the campus, I drove south through town, exploring streets near the college that boast a number of Victorian era homes, including the majestic Stansbury Home at Fifth Street and Salem.

I rejoined Highway 99, which runs north of Chico for about 40 miles on just two lanes of blacktop, ending at Red Bluff, where the old highway joins busy Interstate 5. Along the way I stopped at the little community of Vina for a soft drink at the country store. I also spent some time visiting the monks at the Abbey of New Clairvaux, a Roman Catholic monastery of the Trappist-Cistercian Order. I sat on a stone bench and enjoyed the view of the farmlands worked by the monks. That view today looks out over vineyards, from which the monks produce their award winning wines. The land, once owned by pioneer Peter Lassen and then by the railroad magnate Leland Stanford, became a monastery in 1955. Standford's grand mansion, which stood when I first visited the monastery while a student at Chico State, burned in 1972 and was not rebuilt.

The monastery is now the home of a chapter house, or abbey church, where the monks come together each day for meetings and readings. The church contains the building stones of a chapter house constructed in Spain in the twelfth century. The dismantled stones, purchased by newspaper magnate William Randolph Hearst, were eventually transported to Golden Gate Park in San Francisco, where they remained for decades. Through faith and fundraising, the monks were able to bring the stones to the monastery. The building, with its soaring and arched ceilings, opened to the public in 2012, fully restored to its Gothic glory.

I didn't forget about the Chinese pistache trees. A few weeks after my return home, in late October, I gave a call to Mr. Hodge. "You'd better come soon," Mr. Hodge said. A day later I said goodbye to my wife, dropped my youngest daughter off at school, and hit the road for Chico. It was well after dark when I arrived, so the colorful secrets of the Midway were hidden from me.

The next morning I drove a few minutes from a friend's home, where I'd spent the night, to the Midway, which glowed with colors. The low angle of the sun this late autumn morning made the long, translucent red and orange leaves of the Chinese pistache trees appear as if they were lit by an interior light. Tall and broad, the trees not only lined the Midway, they created a canopy over it perhaps thirty feet high. There were walnut trees, too, their leaves a golden color, the trunks growing in rows on the west side of the old highway. I stopped at Hodge's nursery again and walked across the road to photograph a particularly colorful Chinese pistache, not just red, but crimson. I stopped at the little in Durham bakery for another cup of coffee. Then it was time to begin my trip home. It had been a long trip for one picture, but I didn't regret a minute of it as I headed south on the Midway.

Today, travelers are afforded no views of Durham or the Midway from Highway 99. Nor does the freeway offer a view of Bidwell Mansion, the Esplanade, or the college campus in Chico. Given the amount of traffic on Highway 99, if the freeway hadn't been built, Durham and Chico would be clogged with enormous amounts of traffic. Anyway, few people today want to be diverted by country stores, a walk in the park, a good story, or towns enfolded in the colors of autumn.

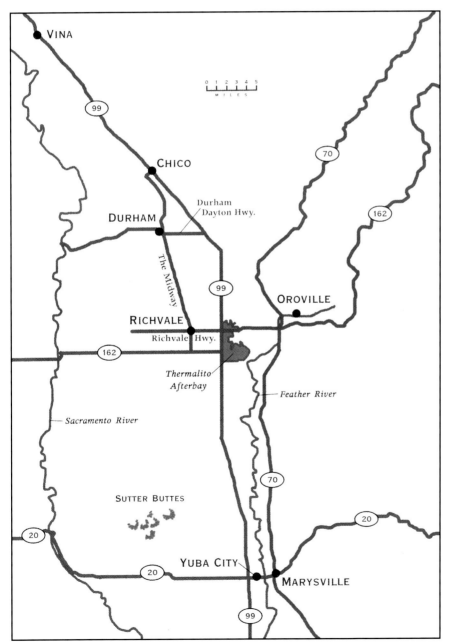

SHUBERT'S ICE CREAM PARLOR IN CHICO.

By David M. Wyman

SEVEN MILES SOUTH OF THE TOWN OF BRIDGEPORT, TURN LEFT OFF OF U.S. HIGHWAY 395 ONTO CALIFORNIA STATE ROUTE 270 (BODIE ROAD). CONTINUE 13 MILES TO BODIE. ALTERNATE ROUTES: 1) FROM BRIDGEPORT, TAKE CALIFORNIA STATE ROUTE 182 ABOUT 4 MILES AND TURN RIGHT ONTO TO MASONIC ROAD. CONTINUE 10 MILES TO BODIE MASONIC ROAD, THEN ANOTHER 7 MILES TO BODIE. 2) FROM THE TOWN OF LEE VINING, TRAVEL NORTH ABOUT 7 MILES AND TURN RIGHT ONTO CALIFORNIA STATE ROUTE 167. DRIVE ABOUT 7 MORE MILES AND MAKE A LEFT TURN ONTO COTTONWOOD CANYON ROAD. CONTINUE 17 MILES TO BODIE.

The
GREAT BASIN
DESERT

BODIE

EARLY MORNING LIGHT FALLS ACROSS SOME OF MONO LAKE TUFA TOWERS AND THE SIERRA NEVADA MOUNTAINS.

AN OLD CAR SITS IN THE MIDDLE OF A GROVE OF ASPENS AT AN EARLY-TWENTIETH-CENTURY MINING SITE OFF MASONIC ROAD.

Ghost towns, ever an endangered species of the American West, are subject to the vicissitudes of old age on the one hand, and vandals on the other. One of the most impressive ghost towns, which goes by the somewhat funny sounding name of Bodie (it rhymes with "toady"), reposes peacefully on the western fringe of the Great Basin desert, east of the Sierra Nevada mountains, and 13 miles off of Highway 395.

It might have a funny name, but there's nothing funny about Bodie's history. It was the reputedly the most violent town in America in the 1870s where, on average, at least one person a day died in a shoot-out or knife fight, from overdosing on alcohol or opium, or in a mining accident.

Gold was the Bodie's chief lure, discovered by Waterman S. Body (also known as William S. Bodey) in 1859. The change in spelling of the town's name was made to insure proper pronunciation. Body froze to death while bringing supplies to his claim before the town that was named for him was built. At its height, over 10,000 people called Bodie home. Residents had to put up with summer temperatures that could rise above 100° F (37°C). Odd as it may seem for a desert environment, the town sometimes had to dig out of winter snow drifts thirty feet deep; temperatures in the minus 20's (-29°C) have been recorded, and winds have been clocked at over 100 miles per hour.

The gold was hauled out of mine shafts sunk deep into the surrounding mountains. Eventually, enormous stamp mills operated 24 ear-splitting hours a day, crushing the rocks and boulders to extract the gold. After 1889, as the gold was depleted, the town began to die.

Bodie is now a state park and is open year-round; a small entrance fee is charged. At more than eight thousand feet above sea level, Bodie is nestled in a high desert valley formed by a spur range of the Sierra Nevada mountains. There are no accommodations or campgrounds, no gas stations or souvenir stands, and not so much as a coke machine. Snow can and often does close the roads, usually from November through May, when the only way to reach the park is on skis or by ski mobile.

When it isn't blocked by snow, Bodie is easy to reach by car. The main road into town, Highway 267, intersects U.S.

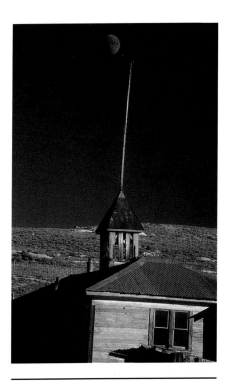

A HALF-MOON RISES OVER THE BODIE SCHOOLHOUSE.

Highway 395 about 10 miles south of the resort town of Bridgeport. It's 13 miles to Bodie, and all but the last 3 miles are paved.

There are two other ways to reach Bodie. One is via Cottonwood Canyon, which begins south of Bodie and is very close to the northern shore of Mono Lake, which features hundreds of "tufa towers," which are weird spires of calcium carbonate that dot the fringes of the lake. (For a close-up view of the tufa, take California State Route 120 east off of Highway 395 for 5 miles to Test Station Road and follow the signs to the lake along a well-graded dirt road leading to a parking lot. Walk about a quarter mile to the edge of the lake.)

Cottonwood Canyon provides a steeper, shorter, rougher route into the park that travels mostly over dirt. However, the road does see less snow than Highway 267. Cottonwood can be reached by turning east off of Highway 395 and onto Highway 167, which is a few miles past the little town of Lee Vining.

The third route to Bodie is my favorite, although it involves a much longer approach and is completely on dirt. Begin about 7 miles north of the little resort town of Bridgeport, and just north of the Bridgeport Reservoir. Turn east off of Highway 395 onto Masonic Road, which is also signed as Forest Service Road 046. The road makes its way up through desert country onto more forested lands, reaching the abandoned Chemung mine about 9 miles from Highway 395. The mine buildings are dilapidated and dangerous to enter, so exercise caution when poking around the site.

The junction with Bodie Masonic Road is a few miles past the Chemung mine. Watch for pronghorn antelope on this stretch of the road. To view the ruins of the Masonic mine, stay left on Masonic Road. It's a mile or so to Masonic, which sits at the bottom of a hill dotted with aspens.

Return to the Bodie Masonic Road, which climbs and drops repeatedly before reaching a plateau. Watch for

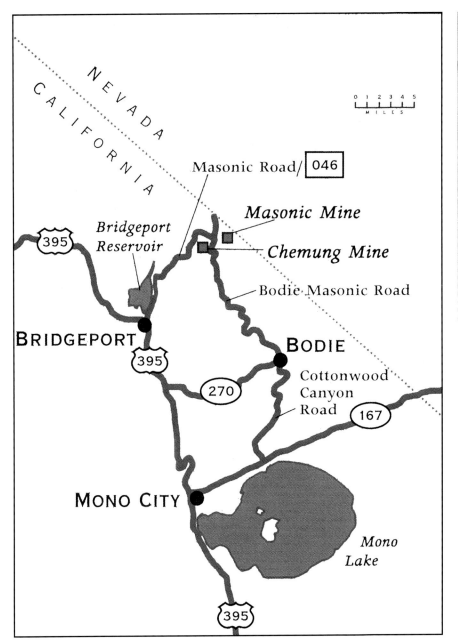

PAINTERLY VIEW OF BODIE, LOOKING THROUGH A LEADED GLASS WINDOW FROM THE STANDARD CONSOLIDATED STAMP MILL.

pronghorn antelope, which put in rare appearances in this rugged terrain. After reaching a plateau, the road begins a final, long descent into Bodie, about 27 miles from its start near the Bridgeport Reservoir.

Bodie comes into view as the road contours around a hillside. Although 85% of the town burned to the ground in two fires, the first in 1892, the last in 1935, Bodie has over five hundred standing or nearly standing structures, including stores, hotels, a saloon, barber shop, the school house, out houses, one of the mills, and private homes, making it the largest, and most authentic ghost town in America.

Today, the danger to Bodie's survival as a ghost town comes from souvenir hunters; board by board and brick by brick, vandals have removed almost every other ghost town that once existed in the western U.S. Park rangers, with the help of infrared burglar alarms, try to keep the tourists honest at Bodie.

Park docents lead tours of some of Bodie's buildings. Visitors are told that Bodie exists in a state of "arrested decay" and they are asked not to touch anything, lest they leave even fingerprints. Even without a tour, it's possible to peer through windows to see hope chests and china sets, schoolbooks, coffins, and a roulette table in the saloon where gambling was conducted illegally, but openly, until 1952.

The only people who stay overnight in Bodie are the rangers and maintenance workers. I skied into Bodie on my first visit, one winter when the snow was especially deep. My companions and I enjoyed a tour led by the two resident rangers. We were, in fact, the only tourists in Bodie. The rangers told us that they had never seen any ghosts but said they had heard odd noises late at night, noises they declined to investigate. They also told us stories about two women, both murdered in the previous century, who had been seen and heard at the upstairs windows of two buildings in recent years. If true, Bodie, the town with the funny sounding name, is indeed a ghost town.

By Karen Misuraca and Gary Crabbe

FROM ARCATA, TAKE U.S. HIGHWAY 101 NORTH TO TRINIDAD, WHERE YOU WILL TAKE STAGECOACH ROAD NORTH. THEN CONNECT TO PATRICK'S POINT DRIVE NORTH AND EVENTUALLY RETURN TO U.S. 101. FROM HERE, CONTINUE NORTH TO ORICK AND PRAIRIE CREEK REDWOODS STATE PARK.

MARSHLANDS, RAINFORESTS, and a ROCKY SEACOAST

ARCATA TO PRAIRIE CREEK STATE PARK

THE ARCATA MARSH REPRESENTS A UNIQUE MODEL WHERE NATURE HANDLES THE FINAL STEPS IN TREATING ARCATA'S CITY SEWAGE, USING PONDS AND REEDS TO CLEANSE THE WATER.

Arcata Marsh and Wildlife Sanctuary on the north end of Humboldt Bay is best seen in the mists of early morning, when stilt-legged herons stand motionless, hidden in the bulrushes. As the air warms, coots mutter and green-winged teal squawk in the narrow canals. Red-winged blackbirds prattle loudly as they cling to the tall reeds, their sharp talons alert for live prey. Northern harriers work the marsh, browsing for voles and squirrels on the pastureland edges. Northern river otters are often seen swimming along in the canals, their heads barely above water, searching for fish, frogs, and turtles—their favorite foods.

The best times of the year to wander the 4 miles of footpaths in the sanctuary are early spring and in November and December, when flocks of migrating ducks and birds number in the thousands. Hundreds of birders are on hand in March for Godwit Days to observe and celebrate the bird that breeds in Alaska and heads south, arriving in the marsh in crowds of twenty thousand or so.

Although it is usually unapparent to visitors, Arcata Marsh is actually a wastewater reclamation project; in fact, it is a model of how to combine wastewater treatment with recreation and wildlife preservation. The city of Arcata also manages the Arcata Community Forest. Established in the 1950s, it was the first city-owned forest in the state. Sustainably logged from time to time, the second-growth redwoods here provide habitat for the endangered spotted owl. Trails for walkers, horseback riders, and bikers wind beneath the towering trees and through fern grottos and meadows.

A few miles north, Trinidad is a seaside village with a small harbor dotted with fishing boats and sheltered on the north end by Trinidad Head, a massive rock outcropping topped by a lighthouse. Fishing for salmon, rockfish, and lingcod is popular off the shore and off the pier or by kayak, by small boat, and on charter boat expeditions. Founded in 1850, Trinidad first boomed during the California Gold Rush and then became a sawmill town

LOW TIDE OFFERS THE CHANCE FOR PEOPLE TO WALK AMONG THE ROCKS AND FIND CREATURES LIKE THESE OCHRE SEA STARS (PISASTER OCHRACEUS) AND A GIANT GREEN SEA ANEMONE AT TRINIDAD STATE BEACH.

THE SKY TRAIL GONDOLA RIDE AT TREES OF MYSTERY—A POPULAR VISITOR ATTRACTION FOR MANY YEARS IN DEL NORTE COUNTY—TRAVELS THROUGH A THICK FOREST TO THE TOP OF A MOUNTAIN.

in the 1870s. In the early twentieth century, it was a busy whaling port, yet today's population only numbers in the hundreds.

Just south of town, travelers veer west from U.S. Highway 101 onto Scenic Road to enjoy the sea views and the series of small beaches. North of town, Patrick's Point Drive is another side road offering a scenic alternate to the main highway. For many miles along this stretch of coastline, dramatic sea stacks, coves, beaches, and headlands compose one of the most magnificent ocean shorelines on the edge of this continent.

About five miles north of Trinidad, Patrick's Point State Park is a square mile of high cliffs; beaches scattered with driftwood; and a forest of fir, pine, and red alder. Visitors can walk on an old Native American trail along the bluffs from which they can spot sea lions, seals, and, in the wintertime, gray whales. At the north end of the park at Agate Beach, tide pools are colorful with

sea anemones, sea stars, and crabs. Bits of jade and agate are often found at the water's edge.

Off U.S. 101 about 6 miles north of Orick is Prairie Creek Redwoods State Park, one of four state parks within Redwood National Park. Prairie Creek's twelve-thousand-acre tract of magnificent coastal redwoods was set aside in the early 1920s. A place of surreal beauty, the park is a dense rainforest that has seldom, if ever, echoed with the sound of an axe or a saw. The forest may seem familiar to moviegoers who saw 1997's The Lost World: Jurassic Park. Backgrounds for the lumbering dinosaurs were filmed here.

The paved Newton B. Drury Scenic Parkway runs ten miles through Prairie Creek, accessing several trailheads along the way. In meadows along the roadside, wild elk herds are often sighted. Fern Canyon, the crown jewel of the park, is a mile-long gorge splitting a coastal

A RECENT ADDITION TO TRINIDAD'S PATRICK'S POINT STATE PARK IS THIS RECONSTRUCTION OF A TRADITIONAL NATIVE AMERICAN YUROK INDIAN LODGE AT SUMEG VILLAGE.

KNOWN FOR ITS STEEP CANYON WALLS AND A POPULAR HIKING SPOT, FERN CANYON IN PRAIRIE CREEK REDWOODS STATE PARK PROVIDES VISITORS WITH A UNIQUE FOREST EXPERIENCE.

bluff and walled by 50-foot cliffs lavishly draped in sword ferns, lady ferns, horsetail, and five-finger ferns. The creamy white bells of fairy lanterns hang in clusters among the greenery. Monkey flowers are flickers of sunny yellow through the dense green. In the wettest areas of the trail, boardwalks and wooden bridges traverse the creeks and marshes. Nearly a foot long, the Pacific giant salamander creeps among the golden globes of the skunk cabbage found here.

The Fern Canyon loop trail connects with a path to Gold Bluffs Beach, which is also accessible by an unpaved road. Bursting out of the canyon as it meets the sea is a profusion of emerald-green ferns, scattered in the spring with wild strawberry blossoms, blue and yellow lupine, and pink rhododendron.

High sandstone cliffs frame 11 miles of driftwood-scattered sand and high dunes. The vigorous surf here creates a vaporous, low-level atmosphere that mingles with the foamy, breaking waves

as they stretch out across sand speckled with real gold, which was mined here in the mid-1800s. Adding to the allure of Gold Bluffs Beach is the sight of grazing Roosevelt elk, which often congregate on clifftops and along the road that runs above the shoreline.

WILD RHODODENDRON FLOWERS ADD A SPLASH OF BRIGHT COLOR TO REDWOOD NATIONAL PARK, DEDICATED IN 1968.

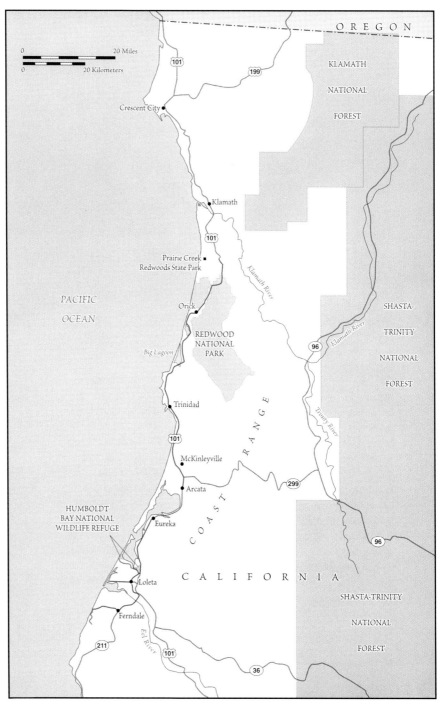

REDWOOD NATIONAL PARK

A UNESCO World Heritage Site, Redwood National Park is one of the last stands of the California coastal redwood. Dedicated in 1968 by President Lyndon B. Johnson, the park shelters half of the remaining old-growth redwoods on earth. The national park actually encompasses three state parks—Prairie Creek Redwoods, Del Norte Coast Redwoods, and Jedediah Smith Redwoods—and includes more than 100,000 acres along 40 miles of coastline. Within the park, visitors will find rivers, streams, hiking trails, campgrounds, and scenic roads.

Flourishing in drizzle and damp, these silent forests resemble a primordial world in which one expects to see pterodactyls flying by. As it is, black ravens do swish through the branches, their shadows flickering in the ancestral gloom. In the understory where the sun breaks through and on the edges of the creeks and rivers, wildflowers and shrubs flourish.

Illuminated by shafts of sunlight glinting through a dense, high canopy, the redwood groves are often described as cathedrals. According to Denise Del Secco, a state park interpretive specialist, "Most people say the same thing when they see the redwoods for the first time: 'awesome.' They do silly things like stand in the middle of the road or walk in circles. . . . People actually get quite overwhelmed at the sight of the tremendous trees."

In drier months, redwoods draw moisture from the air through their boughs, up to a thousand gallons of water a day, one molecule at a time. This adaptation explains, to a degree, why they are able to live on average five hundred to seven hundred years. Some of the trees are more than two thousand years old. Descendants of gigantic evergreens that grew during the age of the dinosaurs and related to the massive giant sequoias found in Kings Canyon, Sequoia, and Yosemite National Parks, redwoods are not as wide or quite as long-lived as sequoias; however, they are considerably taller. Its sapless, cinnamon-colored bark, as much as a foot thick, gives the redwood its distinctive fluted appearance.

In the windy treetops are osprey nests and habitat for two endangered birds: spotted owls and marbled murrelets. Rather than build their own nests, the owls nest in the broken crowns of trees and openings in rotted trunks. About twenty inches (50.8 cm) long with white speckles and brown-colored feathers, they have a sharp hoot that sounds like a small dog barking. Logging roads cut through the mature redwood forests have resulted in the birds' near-extinction.

The most popular destination in the park, Lady Bird Johnson Redwood Grove, is named for one of the leading environmentalists of the twentieth century and lies at the end of a half-mile, old logging road. Standing beneath the towering trees on the occasion of the naming of the grove, Mrs. Johnson said, "Here on the north coast of California, the ancient and awesome redwoods make their last stand. The Latin name for the great redwoods—Sequoia sempervirens—means 'the tree that never dies.' Let us be thankful that in this world, which offers so few glimpses of immortality, these trees are now a permanent part of our heritage."

By Karen Misuraca and Gary Crabbe

FROM U.S. HIGHWAY 101 NEAR MILL VALLEY, TAKE STATE ROUTE 1 (HIGHWAY 1) WEST TO MUIR WOODS, STINSON BEACH, AND BOLINAS, RETURNING TO MILL VALLEY OVER MOUNT TAMALPAIS BY WAY OF THE PANORAMIC HIGHWAY.

The SLEEPING MAIDEN

MUIR WOODS, STINSON BEACH, AND A MOUNT TAMALPAIS LOOP

RISING TO MORE THAN 2,500 FEET IN ELEVATION, MOUNT TAMALPAIS IS THE SENTINEL OF THE NORTH BAY. THE DRIVE TO THE SUMMIT AFFORDS MANY GREAT VISTAS, LIKE THIS SUNSET ON THE HILLS ABOVE THE GOLDEN GATE, LOOKING TOWARD SAN FRANCISCO.

A few miles north of the Golden Gate Bridge, impossible to ignore from any point in Marin County, is the profile of 2,571-foot-tall Mount Tamalpais, sometimes called "the Sleeping Maiden." Sixty-three hundred acres of the mountain is contained in Mount Tamalpais State Park, a verdant world of redwood groves, oak woodlands, grassland slopes, and rocky ridges. On the south side of the mountain, Muir Woods National Monument shelters the last remaining virgin redwood groves in the San Francisco Bay Area. The tallest redwood in the park is 258 feet high and about a thousand years old, still young for redwoods, since they can live for more than two thousand years.

In 2008, the park celebrated the centennial anniversary of President Theodore Roosevelt's declaration that protected this land: "Whereas, an extensive growth of redwood trees embraced in said land is of extraordinary scientific interest and importance because of the primeval character of the forest in which it is located, and of the character, age, and size of the trees, I . . . do hereby declare and proclaim that said grove and all of the land hereinbefore described . . . be set apart as a national monument."

Autumn days in Muir Woods are warm and dry, vivid with maple trees turned gold and fluttering monarch butterflies. Wild azaleas, leopard lilies, and fairybells burst into bloom in the spring, and in the winter, Redwood Creek is in full flood, alive with spawning Coho salmon and steelhead trout. Both are among the West Coast's most imperiled species. Over the last two decades or so, the understory of the woods has been restored with eighty thousand native plants grown from seed collected in the watershed.

Like a mirage, at the end of a steep trail on the edge of the woods is a brightly painted Austrian-style lodge, the Tourist Club. It's operated by Naturfreunde, an international organization of outdoor recreation lovers. Built in the early 1900s by a beloved institution of hikers, the lodge serves imported beers and occasionally puts on alpine festivals with traditional music and dancing.

Below the western slopes of Mount Tamalpais on the Pacific coastline, a tropical undercurrent keeps the waters off Stinson Beach surprisingly warm year-round. Consisting primarily of vacation homes and a short lineup of cafés and a few shops, the village of Stinson Beach is a weekend retreat for San Franciscans escaping the summer fog. Although most Marin County beaches are unsafe for swimming and surfing due to under-tows and currents, Stinson is an exception. Still, the occasional shark sighting does clear the waters of bathers for a day or two at a time.

Stinson Beach residents since the late 1960s, the Arrigoni family fishes not far offshore for salmon every year in their motorboat. Marin historian and author of Making the Most of Marin, Patricia Arrigoni said, "Our sons grew up at Stinson. They waded and swam in the high-tide pools that formed in the fall and winter and caught little perch with their fishing rods.

"Winter is a magical time of year, when thousands of monarch butterflies cluster in the eucalyptus and Monterey pines. We get huge flocks of overwintering birds, especially in the Seadrift Lagoon behind the beach...

We love to watch [the pelicans], with their six-and-a-half-foot wingspans, gliding over the waves, then dive-bombing into the water."

On the opposite side of the Bolinas Lagoon from Stinson Beach, Bolinas is a rustic hamlet inhabited by rogue artists and craftspeople who cut down the road signs regularly to discourage visitors. A few charming nineteenth-century buildings—a couple of cafés, Smiley's Schooner Saloon and Hotel dating from 1851, and St. Mary Magdalene Catholic Church, built in 1878—remain in what passes for a downtown. On Horseshoe Hill in the old cemetery, Catholics, Protestants, and Druids from the mid-1800s have their separate burial grounds.

On the west end of town, Agate Beach is small and rocky, with a footpath leading to Bolinas Lagoon. Its salt marsh and mudflats are a haven for thousands of migrating birds and ducks—as many as thirty-five thousand birds have been spotted here in a single day. One

A NUMBER OF PLACES ON THE CALIFORNIA COAST LEND THEMSELVES TO THE "FEEL LIKE YOU CAN SEE FOREVER" CATEGORY, INCLUDING THIS ONE WHERE A GROUP OF FRIENDS WATCH THE SUNSET AT THE MUIR BEACH OVERLOOK IN MARIN COUNTY.

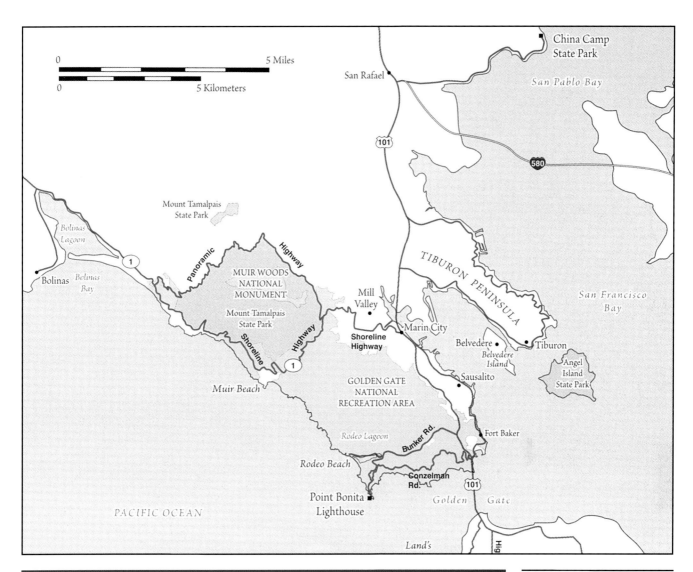

FRESH OYSTERS, A LOCAL DELICACY, ARE HARVESTED FROM ONE OF THE MANY OYSTER FARMS AT SCHOONER BAY IN DRAKES ESTERO ON THE POINT REYES NATIONAL SEASHORE.

MOUNT ST. HELENA RISES IN THE DISTANCE ABOVE ROLLING GREEN HILLS AND TOMALES BAY, AS SEEN FROM POINT REYES NATIONAL SEASHORE. ONLY AN HOUR NORTH OF SAN FRANCISCO, THIS AREA IS BEST KNOWN FOR WIDE-OPEN SPACES, FARMING, AND DAIRY CATTLE.

of the easiest to identify is the glossy black oystercatcher, about seventeen inches (43.2 cm) long with bright red-orange eyes and a long, narrow red bill. Gathering in noisy groups, the birds make shrill whistles—whee-whee-whee—that can be heard above the surf.

Adjacent to the lagoon, the tops of redwoods and pines in the deep canyons of Audubon Canyon Ranch are nesting sites for hundreds of pairs of great blue herons and great egrets. Monarch butterflies spend the winter in a grove of eucalyptus trees along a nature trail outfitted with fixed telescopes for bird-watching. A research station, the ranch is open to the public from March through July on weekends and holidays.

Northwest of Bolinas on Mesa Road, the Point Reyes Bird Observatory is one of America's only full-time ornithological research facilities. Visitors can watch the scientists at work, banding rufous-sided towhees, song sparrows, and other shorebirds. This is also the trailhead for the Palomarin Trailhead, which leads to four freshwater lakes that are lively waterfowl habitats and to Double Point Bay, where harbor seals bask and breed. Just beyond Pelican Lake, a steep canyon trail is generously decorated by the pools and freshets of Alamere Creek, which eventually drops in spectacular style into the sea.

Driving over Mount Tamalpais from the Pacific Coast to U.S. Highway 101, travelers stop near the summit at the Pantoll Ranger Station to browse the small museum and get maps showing 60 miles of trail. An easy hike from here on Old Stage Road/Easy Grade Trail affords wide views, and as the trail connects to the Old Mine Trail, panoramas in all directions are magnificent. On a clear day, you can see the Farallon Islands, about 25 miles out to sea; San Francisco and the bay; the hills and cities of the East Bay; and Mount Diablo. On some occasions, the Sierra Nevada's snow-covered mountains can be seen 150 miles away.

POINT REYES NATIONAL SEASHORE

A glance at a map shows jagged double peninsulas jutting into the Pacific Ocean off the Marin County coastline. An elongated triangle of beaches, lagoons, and estuaries, as well as dark forests and windy headlands, this area is Point Reyes National Seashore, one of the greatest coastal wilderness preserves in the world.

Actually a part of the submerged Pacific continental plate, Point Reyes was once attached to the Tehachapi Mountains, 350 miles to the south. Tectonic movement shoved it north over millions of years, and it is still moving along the San Andreas Fault, which runs through Tomales Bay and down the eastern edge of the park and into the sea. During the 1906 earthquake that devastated San Francisco, the peninsulas moved north twenty feet, an occurrence that is chronicled with photos and signs on the Earthquake Trail near the visitor's center. This land became nationally protected in 1962 by order of President John F. Kennedy.

Set apart from the mainland geologically, and exceptional in their rough beauty, the peninsulas are often wreathed in fog and rudely whipped by Pacific winds. When the English explorer Sir Francis Drake sailed his galleon the Golden Hinde into the great curve of Drakes Bay in 1579, he paused here for a month. He claimed the region for Queen Elizabeth I and named it Nova Albion—meaning new England. A subsequent European mariner, Don Sebastián Vizcaíno, named the land La Punta de los Reyes—The Point of Kings—in 1603.

Due to its inclusion in the national seashore, Drakes Bay remains largely as it was four hundred years ago, fringed with sandy beaches and mottled with deep tide pools alive with anemones, urchins, fish and crabs, leopard rays, and baby sharks. The most developed of the beaches, Drakes Beach is somewhat protected from prevailing north winds by mountainous dunes. The water is too cold and riptides too dangerous for swimming, although body surfers and boogie boarders brave the waves.

On the north end of the bay, surf fishing and sunbathing are the main activities on windswept Limantour Beach. From here, Muddy Hollow Trail traces the edge of Limantour Estero Reserve, a five-hundred-acre intertidal lagoon with a giant tide pool. The smallest North American duck, the striking black-and-white bufflehead, swims about along with common goldeneye ducks, their heads shiny green black with a large round white spot beneath the eye and a dramatic black-and-white body.

Many shipwrecks occurred off Point Reyes until the Point Reyes Lighthouse was built in 1875. Still in operation, the lighthouse is reachable by climbing down more than three hundred steps from a high bluff to the windy Sea Lion Overlook, where most days contingents of sea lions and elephant seals are on view, barking and posing.

Beaches north of the lighthouse are exposed to the full force of storms and pounding surf. Dark pines crowd the headlands above sea stacks and wave-carved caves, and the rocky promontories are alive with birds—brown pelicans, cormorants, surf scooters, sandpipers, grebes, and terns. From February through early summer, meadows and marine terraces are blanketed with California poppies, sky-blue lupine, baby blue-eyes, Indian paintbrush, and some wildflowers existing only here. Often cool and foggy in the summer, the seashore frequently has spring and fall days that are dependably clear and warm. Visitors walk on easy meadow trails, go mountain climbing, bike to the beach, or horseback ride and backpack through this area. The most popular footpath is the Bear Valley Trail.

By Karen Misuraca and Gary Crabbe

FROM PASO ROBLES/HIGHWAY 101, TAKE CALIFORNIA HIGHWAY 46E EAST AS FAR AS TOBIN JAMES WINERY. REVERSE DIRECTION AND FOLLOW 46E WEST, STOPPING AT WINERIES ALONG THE WAY. CROSS U.S. HIGHWAY 101 TO ADELAIDA ROAD, WHICH RUNS WEST TO VINEYARD DRIVE. AT THE INTERSECTION OF ADELAIDA AND VINEYARDS, A SHORT DETOUR NORTH ON CHIMNEY ROCK ROAD LEADS TO JUSTIN VINEYARDS. RETURN TO VINEYARD DRIVE AND HEAD EAST TO TEMPLETON. CROSS U.S. HIGHWAY 101, AND FOLLOW TEMPLE ROAD EAST TO WILD HORSE WINERY.

PASO ROBLES

COWBOY COUNTRY

MORNING FOG ROLLS OVER A VINEYARD AND OAK TREE NEAR PASO ROBLES.

A FAMILY OF BLACK-TAILED DEER WANDERS THROUGH THE COUNTRYSIDE OF SAN LUIS OBISPO COUNTY IN EARLY SPRING.

WISTERIA PLANTS IN BLOOM AT THE MARTIN AND WEYRICH WINERY IN PASO ROBLES.

Settling in the foothills below the dark ridgeline of the Santa Lucia Mountains in the late 1700s, Spanish Franciscan padres built Mission San Miguel Arcángel and planted grapes for their sacramental wines. Decades later, when the Mexican army occupied the area, a land grant called El Paso de Robles—"the pass of the oaks"—was purchased for eight thousand dollars by the Blackburn and James families. In the 1860s, the Southern Pacific Railroad arrived, and the small town of Paso Robles began to grow as headquarters for farmers and ranchers. The town's carefully preserved late-nineteenth-century and early twentieth-century buildings feature a range of architectural styles and today house a lively mix of restaurants, shops, and residences.

More than eighty wineries and over two hundred vineyards thrive within the Paso Robles appellation. Twenty miles inland from the Pacific Ocean, the variation in temperatures is dramatic, with summer days over one hundred degrees and nighttime lows in winter dipping below freezing, with little rain during the growing season. Coastal breezes flow over the Santa Lucia mountain range to cool the vineyards most evenings. Warm-climate reds such as Zinfandel, Cabernet Sauvignon, Merlot, and Rhône-style varieties constitute about 80 percent of the grapes grown here in stony, chalky soil.

In the low hills east of Palo Robles,

Tobin James Cellars harvests Zinfandel grapes from a forty-acre plot of head-pruned, dry-farmed vineyards first planted in 1924. Formerly a stagecoach stop, the winery looks more like a Western saloon than a modern tasting room. Visitors are loudly welcomed up to a rococo, circa-1860 mahogany bar that was shipped from Blue Eye, Missouri. While kids play arcade games, their parents sip and snap photos of Western memorabilia, from six-shooters to saddles, lariats, and horse collars.

A mile or so west on California Highway 46E, Meridian Vineyards is surrounded by a luxuriant herb garden and a grove of ancient oak trees. You can rest here on a bench among the hummingbirds, finches, and frogs,

amid the pungent scent of sage and rosemary, and have a picnic overlooking a reservoir and rows of vines.

Roses line the grand entrance to EOS Estate Winery, founded in the 1980s by former race-car driver, Frank Arciero, Sr. The Romanesque-style stone edifice is meant to be reminiscent of Montecassino, a Benedictine monastery near Arciero's Italian hometown of Sant'Elia Fiumerapido. Besides traditional Paso Robles appellation varieties, EOS produces a unique late-harvest Moscato called "Tears of Dew" and a dated Zinfandel port.

Giant boulders crowd the entrance of cool underground cellars at Eberle Winery. Gary Eberle pioneered San Luis Obispo County winemaking, planting Syrah cuttings brought from France on his Estrella River benchlands in the mid-1970s.

West of Paso Robles is that part of the appellation called the Adelaida, or the "Far Out" wineries region. Not far from the coastline, in rough, rocky terrain and varying elevations and microclimates, a few premium wineries hold forth. Just north of our route on Chimney Rock Road, Justin Vineyards and Winery welcomes visitors for cave tours and tastings of its singular "Isosceles"-style

Cabernets, Syrahs, and Rhône varietals, and its unique Mourvedres and Malbec varietals. Travelers can stay a night or two here at the private French country townhouse, the Vintner's Villa, or at one of the JUST Inn Suites.

When the Mexican army occupied California in the 1820s, it granted expansive ranchos to various local worthies, who established cattle ranches and grain farms. By 1886, the Southern Pacific Railroad was shipping cattle out of the hamlet of Templeton, which began to grow as a supply headquarters and gathering place for the surrounding

area. Today's reminders of the agricultural and ranching history are the towering Templeton Feed and Grain silo, smack in the middle of town. Since 1946 in the building at the base of the silo, livestock feed has been on offer, along with town gossip and friendly banter.

The Templeton Historical Museum Society holds forth on Main Street in a circa-1920 cottage rimmed with white picket fences, where you can see an antique carriage, a 1925 Model T, and inside, local memorabilia and antique photos.

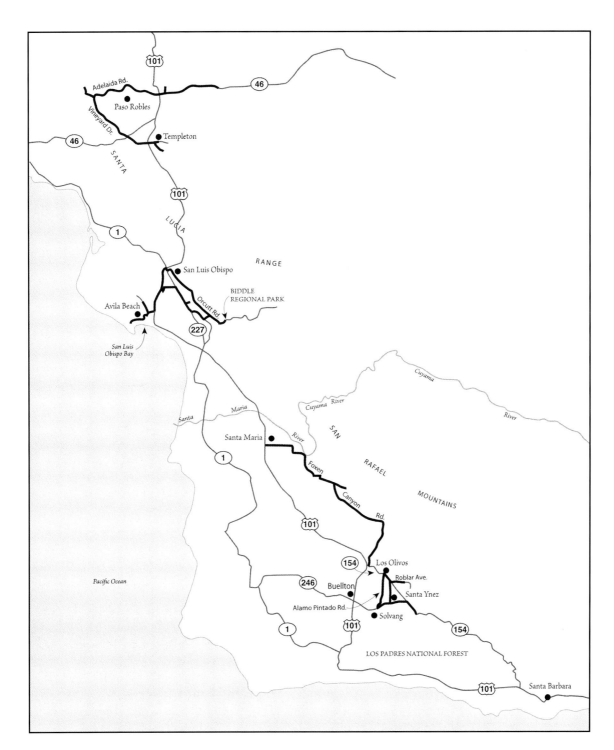

At AJ Spurs Saloon and Dining Hall, you may find yourselves elbow-to-elbow with a cowpuncher in riding boots or a vineyard worker in a wine-stained shirt. A general store and a bank in the 1880s, the building is crowded with Old West memorabilia, from cowhides and spurs to horse collars and old photos.

One of a handful of small wineries on the outskirts of town, Wild Horse Winery on Templeton Road is named for the wild mustangs that once roamed the hills, descendants of the first horses introduced to California by the Spanish in the late 1700s. While most of the award-winning wines here are Pinot Noir, Merlot, Cabernet Sauvignon, Chardonnay, and Viognier, the winery is also known for experimentation with rare varieties such as Malvasia Bianca, Blaufrankisch, and Cheval Sauvage, named, in French, for wild horse.

Chapter 5

UTAH

By Theresa Husarik

FROM INTERSTATE 15, TAKE THE LEHI (STATE ROUTE 73) EXIT AND TRAVEL WEST ABOUT 19 MILES TO FAIRFIELD. JUST BEYOND THE STAGECOACH INN STATE PARK, THE PONY EXPRESS TRAIL LEAVES STATE ROUTE 73. AT THE JUNCTION WITH STATE ROUTE 36, GO LEFT (SOUTH) TO VERNON. TAKE A RIGHT (WEST) ONTO THE SIGNED OLD PONY EXPRESS (DIRT) ROAD. CONTINUE 95 MILES TO IBAPAH, THEN HEAD NORTH ON U.S. HIGHWAY 93 TO INTERSTATE 80.

The
OLD WEST COMES TO LIFE

OLD PONY EXPRESS ROAD

EACH YEAR THE NATIONAL PONY EXPRESS ASSOCIATION HOSTS A RIDE ALONG THE INFAMOUS PONY EXPRESS TRAIL. HERE, A RIDER TAKES A BREAK AT SIMPSON SPRINGS, ONE OF THE ORIGINAL STATIONS ON THE UTAH LEG OF THE JOURNEY.

ONE OF MANY BIRD SPECIES INHABITING UTAH'S
DESERT AREAS, THE BURROW OWL IS UNIQUE IN
THAT IT MAKES ITS HOME IN THE GROUND AND IS
ACTIVE DURING THE DAY.

For mail to get across the West to California before the Pony Express started operating, it traveled by ship down the Gulf of Mexico, by mule across Panama, and then by ship again to San Francisco. That journey could take as long as eight weeks if the weather was foul.

Around the time of the Civil War, it became vital to keep California more closely aligned with the Union, and a faster system for getting messages out was imperative. So in 1860, the Pony Express mail route was born from the vision of businessman William Russell. Starting in St. Joseph, Missouri, the route forged 1,800 miles across what is now Kansas, Nebraska, Colorado, Wyoming, Utah, and Nevada to its terminus in Sacramento, California.

Since speed was the emphasis of this venture, only the fastest horses were used, riders had to weigh less than 120 pounds, and each parcel could be no more than 20 pounds. With the service up and running, the amount of time required to get news to the West Coast was significantly reduced —to about eight to ten days.

Successful as it was, the route was only used for eighteen months, between April 1860 and October 1861. When the transcontinental telegraph was completed in 1861, the privately owned mail delivery business was unable to make a profit and subsequently shut down. Messages that once took eight weeks by ship and mule, then eight days by horse, now took four hours by wire.

But the success of the mail route proved the West could be crossed in all kinds of weather and paved the way for the transcontinental railway.

Travelers today can relive a bit of Old West history by driving what was once the Utah part of that route. Utah's 133-mile long Pony Express Trail National Backcountry Byway begins near Fairfield and ends at Ibapah, near the Utah-Nevada border.

This trip will immerse you in the vast solitude of the Great Basin, a desert region characterized by high elevation and flora and fauna not found in deserts at lower elevations, such as the Bristlecone Pine.

As you drive through the miles and miles of sagebrush country, you can imagine what a day in the life of the riders would have been like: hot and dry in the summer, wet in the spring, and cold in the winter. Regardless of these conditions, frontier-toughened men would ride through the desolate area, stopping at a number of relief stations (roughly 12 miles apart) along the way to refresh themselves and their mounts.

A SUMMER SUNRISE REFLECTS IN A POOL AT FISH SPRINGS NATIONAL WILDLIFE REFUGE.

THE MORMON CRICKET IS A MEMBER OF THE KATYDID FAMILY. EARLY UTAH PIONEERS BELIEVED THE HAND OF THE LORD INTERFERED WHEN A FLOCK OF SEAGULLS SWOOPED IN AND DESTROYED A PARTICULARLY BAD INFESTATION OF THE INSECTS.

The historic Stagecoach Inn State Park in Fairfield is an interesting and informative place to learn more about the history of the route. During its heyday, the inn was an overnight stop for weary travelers along the Pony Express Trail. It is normally open from Easter weekend through October 31.

Fairfield is also the location of Camp Floyd, a former military post named for the 1858 secretary of war, John B. Floyd. Its mission was to establish a military route to California and to suppress a supposed Mormon rebellion in the late 1800s.

When you reach State Route 36, at what is known as Faust Junction, you will see an interpretive marker, erected by the Bureau of Land Management (BLM) in the 1970s with some information about the trail and the relief station that once existed there. There is also a Civilian Conservation Corps (CCC) monument, erected in 1939 to mark the original Pony Express route.

The Lookout Pass station comes next. Long after the Pony Express operation was terminated, the building was adopted as a private home, and the remains of a pet cemetery have been preserved behind a chain-link fence.

Your next stop is at Simpson Springs, another former relief station. A dependable watering hole even today, this area was a popular homestead site where many buildings were erected and subsequently abandoned or destroyed. It is not certain which of the ruins was the actual station building, but the one restored structure sits on a building site dating back to the 1860s. In the 1930s, the CCC established a camp nearby, and in 1965, a monument was erected to mark the site. In the 1970s, the BLM established the area as a camping spot and, in conjunction with Future Farmers of America, finished reconstructing the rock station.

While there were about eighteen stations on this part of the route, there are very few remains. Look for interpretive markers and monuments marking the original route interspersed along the way.

In a few miles, you will come to the Dugway Geode beds. Turn onto the signed road and take a short trip up to an area where you can dig for your own geodes. The best place to find these beautiful and unique specimens is about 1 to 2 miles up this road.

After the geode hunt, come back to the Pony Express road and continue west to Fish Springs Wildlife Refuge, approximately 94 miles from the beginning point of the journey. After so many miles of sagebrush, rocks, and dust, you will be surprised to find this welcoming oasis, which you will likely be able to enjoy all to yourself. Because of the long, desolate, sometimes arduous journey necessary to get there, the refuge is one of Utah's lesser-known wonders.

The ten thousand-acre marsh is divided into nine sections by a gravel road, which makes all the areas very easily viewed by car. The water is so clear that the sandy bottom is always visible, as are the schools of native Utah chub and introduced mosquito fish darting around in the shallows. You can also hear the song of the bull frog and, if you're lucky, maybe spot one.

The best time for seeing abundant birdlife is in the spring and fall during migration. It is rare that you see snow back here, but is a magnificent sight if you are lucky enough to witness it. Snow can make the driving out very hazardous, though, so be careful.

Heading further west the road passes the Deep Creek Mountains, a granite and pine mountain range with 12,000-foot Isapah Peak. The ancient bristlecone pine, known to be several

thousand years old, can be found in these mountains. This is also a great area for viewing wildlife such as Rocky Mountain Bighorn sheep and elk. A large part of this mountain range has been designated as wilderness.

The end point of the Pony Express Trail National Backcountry Byway is at Ibapah, a remote settlement with a quaint trading post. Mormon missionaries originally founded this area in the late 1850s. Here, they taught Native Americans modern farming methods, and later the area housed a Pony Express relief station. The town's name comes from a Goshute Indian word meaning white clay, referring to the white clay deposits found in the water.

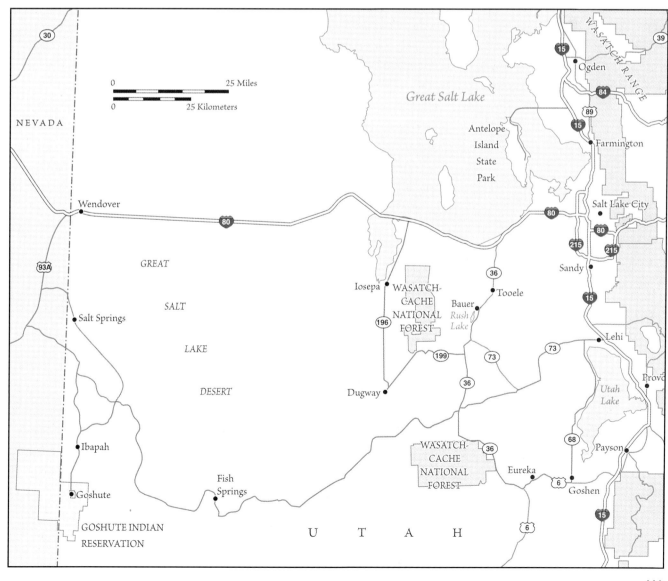

By Theresa Husarik

FROM INTERSTATE 15, TAKE EXIT 112 (IF APPROACHING FROM THE NORTH) OR EXIT 109 (IF APPROACHING FROM THE SOUTH) ONTO BUSINESS 15 (MAIN STREET) IN BEAVER. FOLLOW THIS ROAD UNTIL YOU COME TO THE JUNCTION WITH STATE ROUTE 153 AND FOLLOW ROUTE 153 INTO THE BEAVER CANYON. CONTINUE ON THIS ROAD THROUGH THE CANYON TO THE JUNCTION WITH U.S. HIGHWAY 89 IN THE TOWN OF JUNCTION. TAKE A SIDE JAUNT SOUTH ON HIGHWAY89 TO BUTCH CASSIDY'S BOYHOOD HOME IN CIRCLEVILLE, THEN HEAD NORTH ON HIGHWAY 89 TO ITS JUNCTION WITH INTERSTATE 70.

BUTCH CASSIDY was HERE

BEAVER CANYON TO I-70

AUTUMN COLORS REFLECT IN THE GLASSY WATERS OF KENT'S LAKE.

THE REMAINS OF THE HOUSE WHERE BUTCH
CASSIDY SPENT HIS TEENAGE YEARS BEFORE
HITTING THE ROAD ON HIS INFAMOUS JOURNEY
TO OUTLAW HISTORY.

This beautiful drive winds through the Tushar Mountain Range and the Fishlake National Forest, providing magnificent scenery and loads of recreational opportunities. The usual summer fun activities—camping, fishing, hiking, and horseback riding—abound here, as do winter sports like snowmobiling and skiing.

At an elevation of 5,970 feet, Beaver, the starting point of this route, is a place with a colorful past, a pleasant climate, and several points of interest to explore. It is the birthplace of Butch Cassidy, the infamous Old West outlaw, as well as Philo T. Farnsworth, the inventor of the television.

Formally incorporated in 1867, Beaver is known for its stone houses, built from the black rock found in the area. The town's courthouse, whose foundation was built in 1882 with the indigenous black rock, remains one of the county's most prominent landmarks.

The U.S. Army built a military barracks at Beaver in 1872, also using the distinctive black rock. These barracks remained occupied until 1883. The buildings of Fort Cameron (named after Colonel James Cameron, who was killed in the battle at Bull Run) were later used as the Beaver branch of the Brigham Young Academy (later renamed Brigham Young University). In 1922, the Utah state legislature passed a law requiring all Utah counties to maintain tuition-free high schools, and after twenty-five years, the academy was closed. Much of the land was sold and the equipment donated to the new Beaver High School. Eventually most of the land was sold, and most of the buildings were razed—except one that is currently a private residence. The marker on the corner of the road at the beginning of State Route 153 commemorates this bit of history.

At mile marker 10 on State Route 153, there is a turnoff to Kent's Lake, a great fishing hole in the forest where you can catch rainbow, brook, and brown trout. Camping and hiking are also part of the summertime recreation here. Puffer Lake, a few more miles down the road, is also a good place to catch trout and enjoy the scenery.

What used to be Elk Meadows Ski and Summer Resort is up ahead. The resort recently shut its doors, and the land was sold to a developer. It is not known what will become of the resort, but the nearby forest area with its peaks reaching over twelve thousand feet (towering to 12,169 feet, Delano Peak is the seventh highest peak in Utah) is a beautiful sight to see. The road itself summits at ten thousand feet.

Just past Puffer Lake, the pavement ends. The dirt road that continues is drivable with a passenger car (no four-wheel-drive needed) and continues over vast expanses of meadows and crosses the Paiute ATV trail. This 238-mile loop through rugged yet beautiful terrain was rated one of the fifteen best ATV trails in America by *Dirt Wheels* magazine.

As the road nears the junction with U.S. Highway 89 at the town of Junction, Utah, you go down a series of switchbacks through a steep mountainside. Beautiful views of the valley floor can be enjoyed from the top of the descent.

Once you reach U.S. Highway 89, take a side jaunt down to Circleville to see the boyhood home of Butch Cassidy. Between mile markers 156 and 157, this wooden structure in disrepair is a piece

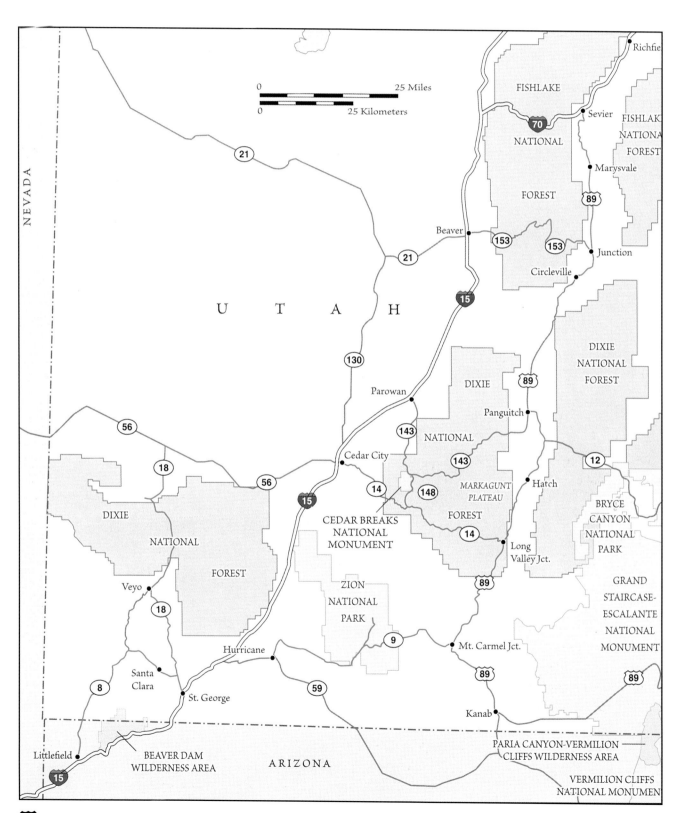

of history for both Utah and the Old West. Butch Cassidy (nee Robert LeRoy Parker) lived here from the time he was thirteen years old until he moved away in his late teens and began his career in crime.

The stretch of U.S. Highway 89 that goes north to Interstate 70 and the end of this route goes through a mixture of farmland and rocky canyons. A rest area at Big Rock Candy Mountain, named because of its resemblance to the sweet treat, is a nice place to stop for a snack and to read the interpretive signs about the area.

AN OLD LOG FENCE AND COLORFUL ASPEN TREES MAKE FOR A PEACEFUL SIGHT NEAR KENT'S LAKE IN BEAVER CANYON.

BUTCH CASSIDY AND UTAH

The infamous Butch Cassidy (nee Robert LeRoy "Roy" Parker), outlaw of the Old West, was born on April 13, 1866, in Beaver, Utah. When he was thirteen, his family moved to Circleville on the other side of the mountain range. The house he lived in there still stands today.

Butch Cassidy got his place in outlaw history as a thief (in those days the term used was "robber") and his forte was trains, banks, and horses.

He started a gang that was called "The Wild Bunch" (which included his sidekick Harry Longabaugh, the "Sundance Kid"). The gang was very successful and terrorized the people of the western states for many years.

The legacy of his career in crime is renowned, but where he actually died is a subject that has been questioned. The official story goes that he died in South America, where he fled when U.S. law officials closed in on him.

But some of the people who knew him say different; they claim he came back to the states, cleaned up his act, and lived out the rest of his life an honest man.

Several museums around southern Utah (such as the Butch Cassidy Museum in Richfield and also in Circleville, and the Western Mining and Railroad Museum in Helper) preserve some of the relics and stories of Utah's infamous native son.

By Theresa Husarik

START AT STATE ROUTE 12'S WESTERN ENDPOINT AT THE JUNCTION WITH U.S. HIGHWAY 89. CONTINUE EAST TO THE ROUTE 12'S EASTERN ENDPOINT IN TORREY.

All-
AMERICAN
ROAD
STATE ROUTE 12

SCENIC STATE ROUTE 12, AN ALL-AMERICAN ROAD, CUTS THROUGH THE SANDSTONE OF ESCALANTE NATIONAL MONUMENT.

State Route 12, designated an All-American Road in 2002, winds 124 miles through some of the most unique geology on earth. It also connects two national parks, several state parks, wilderness areas, and offers views beyond belief. One of the best things about this road is that the terrain just keeps changing, and some of the vistas go on for miles.

Heading east, you first come to Red Canyon, a section of the Dixie National Forest that sports red hillsides dotted with ponderosa pine trees. Several hiking trails, a biking path, a campground, and a visitor's center make this a great place to stop and explore.

After about 14 miles on this road, you come to the turnoff to Bryce Canyon National Park. Named after Mormon pioneer Ebenezer Bryce (before its designation as a national park, the area was referred to by the locals as Bryce's canyon), the canyon's hoodoos (redrock spires) are concentrated in horseshoe-shaped amphitheaters that provide amazing spots to watch the sunset and

sunrise. Since the area is so far from a large city, and all a city's light sources and pollution, the park is also a great place for stargazing. And on a clear day, you can see mountaintops 200 miles away. Several hikes and horseback riding trails go down among the spires with names like Thor's Hammer, Inspiration Point, Fairyland Canyon, and the Hat Shop.

Continuing on State Route 12, you enter the Grand Staircase–Escalante National Monument with geology spanning eons of time and an enormous potential for recreational opportunities. Several four-wheel-drive roads are here, as well as the roaring Escalante River and several trails leading to geologic features and Native American artifacts and ruins. From here until you reach the town of Boulder, you will be traveling through this monument.

Among the many points of interest in the monument are Devils Garden (an area where visitors can climb on the rocks and walk along petrified sand dunes), the Hole-in-the-Rock Road

(where the Mormon pioneers crossed through a narrow passageway in their quest to go west), Dance Hall Rock (a large sandstone outcropping), the Peek-a-Boo slot canyon, and Coyote Gulch hiking trail (one of my most favorite backpack trips ever).

Kodachrome Basin State Park can be reached by a spur road in Cannonville. The brightly colored sand pipes (or petrified geysers) inspired the National Geographic to come up with its name. About 10 miles southeast of this park, you will see Grosvenor Arch, a sandstone structure jutting up from the valley floor and arching over about sixty feet of open air.

Just past Henrieville is an area called The Blues, which is an elk migration corridor. Watch for these and other wildlife, especially in the fall and winter.

The town of Escalante, settled in 1876, was named after a Spanish priest who was with a party believed to be one of the first white people to set foot in the area in 1776. Legend has it during the settlers' first Fourth of July in the valley, they didn't have an American flag, so they raised a striped Navajo blanket instead.

An interesting side trip here is to go up the Hell's Backbone Road (also known as Salt Gulch) that loops from Escalante just south of the town of Boulder. The road passes through the Dixie National Forest and the Box-Death Hollow Wilderness. The Hell's Backbone Bridge, built in the 1930s by the Civilian Conservation Corps, spans the narrow head of Death Hollow and Sand Creek. The views here are stunning.

As you leave Escalante, you pass several lookout points and cross over the area called the Hogback. When you drive over it, you will understand how it got its name. The very narrow ridge (in some places it is just wide enough for a two-lane road) with a deep canyon on either side is not for the faint of heart. Stop at one of the many pullouts along the ridge and gaze at the sheer cliffs that tumble hundreds of feet below.

The Calf Creek Recreation Area is a few miles south of Boulder. The center point of this southern Utah landmark is the Lower Calf Creek Falls, which can be reached by an easy 2.75-mile hike.

THE EASY TRAIL OUT TO THE 126-FOOT LOWER CALF CREEK FALLS PASSES THROUGH BEAUTIFUL REDROCK COUNTRY AND SOME ROCK ART AND THEN ENDS IN A LUSH GREEN RIPARIAN OASIS.

THE HISTORIC SIGNIFICANCE OF THE HOLE IN THE ROCK ROAD

In 1879 and 1880, church leaders called Mormon settlers to leave Escalante and settle the country in Southeast Utah, near what is now known as the city of Bluff. Scouts took several months to find the best route, and even then the one they chose had some major obstacles. It had several ravines and washes that had to be crossed, steep cliffs, and dry and rocky terrain. And then there were the sheer cliff walls that needed to be crossed to get to the Colorado River. But the group decided the route was passable, and it set out.

When the settlers reached the 1,200-foot cliffs at the river, there was not an easy way down for climbers, let alone all the wagons and livestock. But the settlers were on a mission; failure was not an option. So they labored for about six weeks, chiseling and blasting a passage big enough to allow them to lower the wagons.

They named the passage the Hole in the Rock, and the area is still visited today. It is located down a dirt road about 57 miles southeast of Escalante.

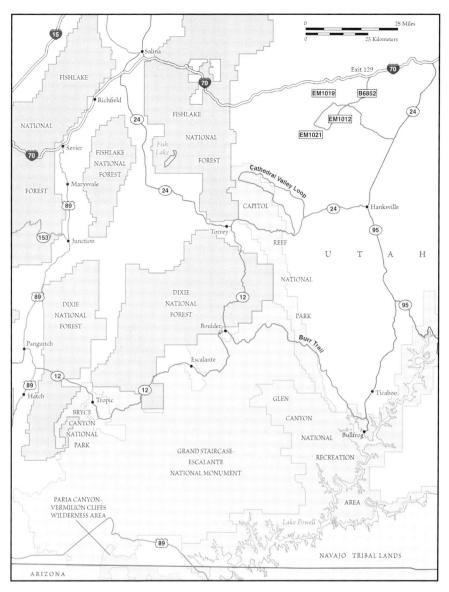

In summer, the pool at the bottom of the falls is a popular place for the weary hiker to cool off after a hot walk. There is also an upper falls, a little harder to get to, but also very scenic.

Boulder, a green-pastured oasis with natural artisan springs surrounded by 500-foot white cliffs of sandstone, is one of the most beautiful towns in America. Several of the residents are direct descendants of original settlers to the area. Also known as the "last frontier in Utah," the town was the last one in the United States to receive mail by mule. The road was so rough that milk and cream carried by mule turned to butter before it could arrive at the intended destination.

The name of this area is the Aquarius Plateau and is geologically significant in that it is the highest and largest of southern Utah's high plateaus. Boulder Mountain is part of this region.

Also known as the Land of a Thousand Lakes, the mountain is a fisherman's dream with numerous trophy trout living in its waters. Several established forest service campgrounds high on the mountainside make this a great place to camp in the heat of the summer. In the fall, the colors are astonishing and views from the many lookout points will inspire all. This section of State Route 12 was unpaved until 1985.

The road then heads back down the mountain and into the town of Torrey, then end of this route.

By Theresa Husarik

Along the MIGHTY COLORADO

POTASH ROAD TO DEAD HORSE POINT

BATHED IN EARLY-MORNING SUNLIGHT, TURRET ARCH IN ARCHES NATIONAL PARK CAN BE SEEN IN THE PARK'S WINDOWS SECTION.

ABOUT 2 MILES NORTH OF THE TOWN OF MOAB ON U.S. HIGHWAY 191, TAKE STATE ROUTE 279 SOUTH AND WEST. DRIVERS WITH HIGH-CLEARANCE AND FOUR-WHEEL-DRIVE VEHICLES CAN CONTINUE AFTER THE PAVEMENT ENDS UP THE SHAFER TRAIL TO STATE ROUTE 313. AFTER ABOUT 5 MILES ON SHAFER TRAIL, FOLLOW THE DEAD HORSE POINT ROAD INTO THE POINT. FROM THE POINT, GO BACK OUT TO STATE ROUTE 313 AND HEAD EAST TOWARD HIGHWAY 191. PASSENGER VEHICLES: WHEN YOU GET TO THE END OF THE PAVEMENT AT THE SALT PLANT, BACKTRACK OUT TO U.S. HIGHWAY 191. HEAD NORTH ON HIGHWAY 191 TO STATE ROUTE 313 AND DRIVE OUT TO THE DEAD HORSE POINT ROAD AND DOWN TO THE POINT.

Paralleling the Colorado River for about 17 miles, this route travels through towering redrock walls that hug the road. Several spots along the way are popular for rock climbing, and you may even see a rugged individual or two hanging from a rope way up high on the cliff or climbing up the sheer wall seemingly with ease.

Along the way, you shortly come to the Jaycee Park recreation site with some campsites and a 1.5-mile trail to the Portal Overlook, with panoramic views of the Moab Valley, the La Sal Mountains, and the Colorado River.

After about 5 miles in, you come to a spur road going up a short hill. At the top of this hill is a parking lot holding cars of the mountain bikers who came to test their mettle on the Poison Spider Mesa trail. This popular bike and four-wheel-drive trail is only for the most daring of drivers and riders, and it is a good representation of what navigating a vehicle on gonzo abusive slickrock is like.

Also at the parking lot, you can see some fossilized dinosaur tracks, as well as a good petroglyph panel in the rock above. Interpretive signs point out where they are and a spotting tube has been installed down near the road for those who need help finding the tracks.

About 10 miles in, you come to the Bowtie and Corona Arch trailhead. Corona Arch has the distinction of having been flown through—yes, a local pilot was brave enough to fly a small plane through the 140 foot by 105 foot opening. Then after another 4 miles, you come to Jughandle Arch, an opening high on the rock wall, so named because it is forty-six feet high and only three feet wide. Shortly after this arch, the rock walls recede a bit and the desert scenery opens up into some expansive views of the Colorado Plateau and Canyonlands National Park.

BROKEN ARCH IS SO NAMED BECAUSE OF THE CRACK-LIKE FOLD IN ITS CENTER. IT CAN BE REACHED AFTER A SHORT WALK FROM THE CAMPGROUND IN ARCHES NATIONAL PARK.

THE HUGE BRILLIANT BLUE
EVAPORATING PONDS CREATED IN
THE POTASH MINING PROCESS CAN
BE VIEWED FROM DEAD HORSE
POINT. *SHAWN MITCHELL PHOTO/
SHUTTERSTOCK*

THE CACTUS FLOWER HAS DELICATE
PETALS, IN STARK CONTRAST TO ITS
SURROUNDING SPINES.

The Moab Salt Plant sits at the end of the pavement, at about 17 miles in. Moab has been involved in the mining industry since even before its humble beginnings in Utah. Incorporated in 1903, Moab became known as the uranium capital of the world in the 1950s and was home of the nation's second largest uranium processing mill (the tailings from this mill are still visible from the highway.) Next came a mini oil boom that lasted into the 1960s. In the 1960s, mining potash became lucrative, and a modern potash plant and a railroad spur from the D&RGW at Crescent Junction to service the plant were built here. Potash is used in fertilizer and is mined via an elaborate process using a lot of water, an extensive tunnel system, and evaporating ponds. These ponds with their crystal blue color can be viewed from Dead Horse Point (the end of this trip.)

The potash plant is the end of the road for those who do not have high-clearance and four-wheel-drive vehicles. To see Dead Horse Point, take the alternate route described in the route directions.

For those who are up for the off-road part of this trip, there are some beautiful sites to see ahead as you travel through the backcountry areas of Canyonlands National Park. You will pass by the towering cliffs of Dead Horse Point and a section of the White Rim Trail (the first route in this section) for a little while.

Getting back to pavement involves ascending the Shafer Trail, a series of tight switchbacks going up a steep cliffside that should only be attempted in good weather. If you get to the bottom and the road is too muddy, turn around and go back out the way you came in.

At the top of Shafer Trail, this road ends and you run into State Route 313, which leads to the road out to Dead Horse Point. This strange name for such a beautiful place came about after a tragedy.

Wild mustangs once roamed freely in this area, until local cowboys started rounding them up, breaking them in, and either keeping or selling the best

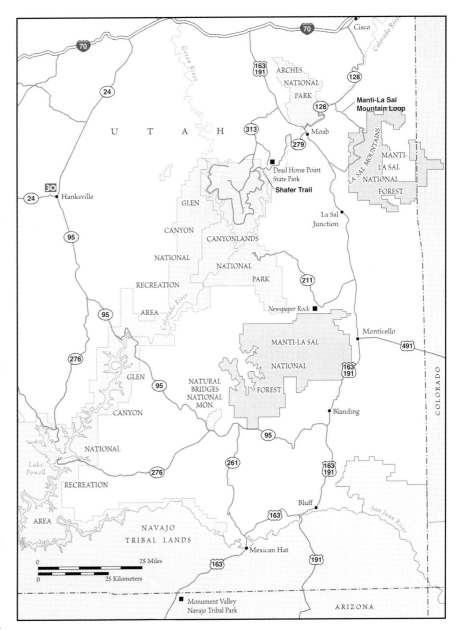

ones. The narrow passageway leading to the point made for a convenient natural corral. Only a small barrier was needed to keep the animals caged in and it was easily constructed by using sticks and brush.

Legend has it that on one occasion, the cowboys took the horses they wanted but then forgot to open the gate allowing the less desirable ones to go wild again. Unable to get out, the horses died of thirst, within view of the waters of the Colorado River two thousand feet below.

After contemplating this tragic story, walk around the point for some astounding views of the Colorado River, the potash plant evaporating ponds, and the road you just traveled to get here.

By Theresa Husarik

COWBOYS and INDIANS,

BOTH PAST AND PRESENT

TRAIL OF THE ANCIENTS SCENIC BYWAY

ARTIST ALBERT CHRISTENSEN AND HIS WIFE, GLADYS, SPENT 12 YEARS BLASTING THROUGH SOLID ROCK, ENDING UP WITH A 5,000-SQUARE-FOOT HOME THEY NAMED HOLE 'N THE ROCK. THE PLACE OFFERS TOURS THROUGH THE CAVE AND IS HOME TO AN EXTENSIVE COLLECTION OF METAL SCULPTURES.

STARTING IN MOAB, HEAD SOUTH ON U.S. HIGHWAY 191 TO THE JUNCTION WITH U.S. HIGHWAY 163, 4 MILES WEST OF BLUFF. AT THIS JUNCTION, HIGHWAY 191 MAKES A SHARP TURN TO THE SOUTH AND HIGHWAY 163 GOES SOUTH AND WEST. TAKE HIGHWAY163 TO THE UTAH-ARIZONA BORDER AND THE EDGE OF MONUMENT VALLEY TRIBAL PARK. HEAD BACK UP HIGHWAY163 TO THE JUNCTION WITH STATE ROUTE 261 AND GO NORTHWEST. JUST A COUPLE OF MILES AFTER GETTING ONTO ROUTE 261, TAKE THE SPUR ROAD OUT TO GOOSENECKS STATE PARK. CONTINUE NORTH ON STATE ROUTE 261 TO ITS END AT STATE ROUTE 95.

Named the Trail of the Ancients because of the rich Native American history found along the way, this scenic byway also travels through an area full of pioneer history and recreational points of interest. Parts of the official trail head into Colorado, but this route will only discuss the Utah section.

Inhabited by the Anasazi around ten thousand years ago, the area today is home to both Ute and Navajo communities. At several places along the route, you may see roadside stands where the locals sell their southwest art (pottery, jewelry, rugs) directly to the public.

One of the first points of interest as you head south is a tourist attraction called the Hole 'N the Rock. Not the area in Escalante with a similar name (described in Part V), this hole was excavated for a different purpose. Artist Albert Christensen and his wife Gladys spent twelve years blasting through the solid rock and ended up with a 5,000-square-foot home where they lived together until Albert died in 1957. Gladys turned the front part into

BLUFF WAS ORIGINALLY BUILT AS A FORT AND CONSISTED OF JUST A FEW BUILDINGS. AS THE TOWN PROSPERED, THE ORIGINAL BUILDINGS WERE TORN DOWN AND THEIR STONES USED IN NEW PROJECTS. WHAT REMAINS ARE THE RUINS OF ONE OF THE EARLY HOUSES AND A RESTORED CABIN CONTAINING ARTIFACTS SHOWING WHAT LIFE WAS LIKE IN THOSE EARLY DAYS.

THE EDGE OF CEDARS STATE PARK IN BLANDING HAS GREAT EXAMPLES OF PRESERVED ANASAZI RUINS. VISITORS CAN EXPLORE THEM AND DESCEND INTO A KIVA VIA A LADDER.

a museum and lived there, giving tours until her death in 1974. Tours are still given today, and an extensive collection of metal sculptures and a petting zoo are on the grounds.

Wilson Arch is a little further down the road. Named after a local homesteader, this 6,155-foot arch is just off the highway and provides a fun yet invigorating hike with some bird's eye views of the surrounding areas.

After about 40 miles on this road, you come to the turnoff for the Indian Creek Corridor route. Right across the street from where that route takes off is a neat rock formation called Church Rock that looks like a domed cathedral. A rounded cave at ground level looks like it could be an immense church door. This formation is behind private property, so closer investigation is not possible.

The visitor's center in Blanding has a nice museum with artifacts and stories of the area's early days, and Edge of the Cedars State Park, also in Blanding has some great examples of preserved Anasazi ruins where visitors can actually descend into a kiva via a ladder.

The town of Bluff was settled by those who came from Escalante via the infamous Hole-in-the-Rock Trail. Historic Bluff Fort has some preserved buildings, a covered wagon, and interpretive signs.

A section of the Trail of the Ancients heads east from Bluff, where, if you have the time and inclination, you can explore Hovenweep National Monument, a park known for its uniquely shaped towers. A walkway takes interested visitors around several well-preserved remains of Anasazi structures. Continue further along and into Colorado where you can get to the Four Corners Monument, a tribal park located on Navajo land.

Just outside of Bluff is the Sand Island recreational area with San Juan River access and a large petroglyph panel.

On the way to the Utah-Arizona border, take the spur road out to the Mexican Hat rock formation, after which the town of Mexican Hat was named.

After passing through some very remote countryside with Native American communities scattered throughout, you come to the Utah border and the entrance to the Monument Valley Tribal Park. A sort of strip mall of makeshift shelters houses several shops selling Navajo jewelry and pottery. The locals are very friendly and love to talk about their culture. The iconic rock formations in the park (across the border in Arizona) have served as a backdrop for countless Western movies.

Heading back northward, near the junction with State Route 261, take the spur road out to Gooseneck State Park with views of the meandering San Juan River one thousand feet below.

The last viewpoint on our trip is the Valley of the Gods, a remote area with rock formations similar to Monument Valley, but on a smaller scale. The road winds one thousand feet up a series of switchbacks called the Moki Dugway, giving some incredible views, and it then winds through pinion and juniper forests to its end at State Route 95.

Just before this route's end is the Grand Gulch Primitive area, a popular yet remote hike to several good examples of Anasazi ruins and rock art. Some of the sites can be seen with just a day hike, but to really explore, a multiple-day backpack venture is recommended. Permits are required for overnight stay.

A NATIVE AMERICAN RIDES HIS HORSE ACROSS A BLUFF WITH THE MITTENS OF MONUMENT VALLEY IN THE DISTANCE.

THE SLICKROCK BIKE TRAIL

Perhaps the most popular mountain biking trail in the world, the Slickrock Bike Trail is one of the reasons Moab is considered a mecca for mountain biking worldwide. First used by motorcyclists, the trail has become the place to show your mastery of muscle and fat tire versus rocks and sand.

Bike manufacturers try out new equipment here regularly since the terrain will push the limits of any human-bike combination. You wouldn't think a mere 12 miles could wear out even those in tip-top shape, but the trail's grueling technical nature necessitates slower and more careful riding. For those who want to

try the trail without the average four-hour commitment, there is a 2.3-mile practice loop.

Besides all this technical riding, the trail affords spectacular views of Arches National Park and the La Sal Mountains, as well as some of its own interesting rock formations and canyons.

Chapter 6

OREGON

FIREWEED BLOOMS NEAR THE YAQUINA HEAD LIGHTHOUSE, JUST NORTH OF NEWPORT, OREGON. *BOB POOL/ SHUTTERSTOCK*

By Rhonda and George Ostertag

THIS ROUTE IS A 106-MILE SAMPLE OF THE PACIFIC COAST SCENIC BYWAY, WHICH FOLLOWS U.S. HIGHWAY 101 FROM THE COLUMBIA RIVER TO THE CALIFORNIA BORDER; THIS SNAPSHOT RUNS BETWEEN LINCOLN CITY AND REEDSPORT.

All THINGS COASTAL

LINCOLN CITY TO REEDSPORT

THE VIEW NORTH FROM ROADS END STATE PARK IN LINCOLN CITY INCLUDES THIS POPULAR WALKING BEACH, WHERE BEACHCOMBERS CAN FIND AGATES AND SOMETIMES A HANDSOME BLOWN-GLASS FLOAT.

Oregon's coast is legendary, rolling out sandy strands, rocky headlands, rumpled dunes, tidepools, and an always mesmerizing surf. Nesting seabirds, bald eagles, sea lions, spouting gray whales, and even the occasional orca endorse the stage. But, the coast's invitation extends beyond its natural offering, with a rich maritime lore, fun-in-the-sun coastal shops, salty bay fronts, chainsaw art, battling kites, and castles in the sand.

In 1913, Oregon Governor Oswald West declared the coastal beaches highways—an action that kept the beaches public and undeveloped. Historically, the beaches were the lone transportation links between isolated coastal communities, and they were used by both Native Americans and pioneers. What beachgoers today reap is 363 miles of unprecedented access to natural shores. Some beaches have shell fossils (Moolack Beach), some have agates (Lost Creek), and some are untrammeled canvases.

Lincoln City launches this trip. This linear town incorporates five former beach communities. It is known for its spring and fall kite festivals and its winter treasure hunts of blown-glass floats hidden on the beaches. By contrast, its little sister to the south, Depoe Bay, is a compact seafront village, where fishing and whalewatching charters enjoy a quick hop to the open ocean through the world's smallest port.

State parks, beaches, and waysides pepper the length of the coast allowing frequent stops and tastes of the sea breeze. The ocean mirrors the weather; it can be as striking blue as the sky, or as moody and mysterious as the fog. Wind is common anytime; best weather comes in fall.

Newport's waterfront smacks of the sea, with its circling gulls, barking sea lions, stacked crab rings, and old warehouses. A series of marine-inspired murals and an inviting seawalk further put visitors in a nautical mood. The historic fishing village remains home to one of Oregon's largest commercial fishing fleets, and tuna still can be bought fresh off the boat. For alternative windows to the sea, visitors may look to the Oregon Coast Aquarium and Hatfield Marine Science Center.

What would a visit to the coast be without foghorns and lighthouses? Newport boasts a pair of lighthouses. The misplaced Yaquina Bay Lighthouse, on the harbor in town, was used only three years but comes complete with ghost story. Its replacement, the 1873 Yaquina Head Lighthouse (at the north end of town) shines over Yaquina Head Outstanding Natural Area; it is the tallest of the nine remaining Oregon lighthouses, standing 93 feet tall.

ALONG THE OLD-TIME WATERFRONT OF NEWPORT,
NAUTICAL-THEMED MURALS ADORN WAREHOUSES
AND SHOPS.

Off Yaquina Head sits Colony Rock, a nesting site for thousands of common murres, Brandt's and Pelagic cormorants, and pigeon guillemots. April through July, it's standing room only for the colony, unless the bald eagles stir things up. Nesting gulls prefer the headland cliff. The headland also serves leviathan seekers. Of the dozen species of cetaceans, whales, dolphins, and porpoises, spied off the Oregon coast, gray whales account for 95 percent of sightings.

The tiny town of Yachats heralds one of Oregon's more spectacular rock-and-sea clashes. At Smelt Sands State Recreation Site, fingers of jet-black basalt confront the white fury of the sea in high-spraying spectacle. Winter storms feed the fury, and thunder rumbles in the chests of onlookers.

To its south looms Cape Perpetua, named by Captain James Cook in 1778. Cape Perpetua Scenic Area encompasses this rugged headland, wild coast, forest, and 22 miles of hiking trails. Adjoining Cummins Creek Wilderness to the south, the scenic area shapes a large open-space for wildlife. The summit's Whispering Spruce Trail links two stonework vantages built by the Civilian Conservation Corps. Shoreline attractions Devils Churn, Cook's Chasm, Spouting Horn, and Thor's Well (a photographers' favorite) live up to their provocative names.

The signature flashes of Heceta Head Lighthouse call travelers south. Its stunning coastal perch makes this the state's most photographed lighthouse. Two-hundred-foot cliffs, the rocky cove of Devils Elbow, and the sea-battered Conical and Parrot Rocks shape the light's dominion. The associated lightkeeper's house doubles as an interpretive center and bed and breakfast.

Raucous barks announce the nearness of the Steller sea lion rookery at privately held Sea Lion Caves. According to the owners, this gaping 12-story-high cavern spans the length of a football field—plenty of room for beasts that can weigh one ton each. An elevator sinks 208 feet to the cave floor for viewing this wildlife spectacle.

Elsewhere along the coast, smaller, more common California sea lions frequent docks and waterfronts, and harbor seals sun themselves on isolated rocks.

Wrapping up the journey, the cities of Florence and Reedsport shape the northern gateway to Oregon Dunes National Recreation Area, which stretches nearly 50 miles between Florence and Coos Bay. The origin of the dunes traces back 7,000 years. Over time, sand slowly eroded from the interior mountains and rode the rivers to the sea, where currents distributed the deposits along the shoreline. At the end of the last Ice Age, a bulldozing wave action pushed the sand to shore. Centuries of wind then finessed the shifting landscape. The resulting curvaceous dunes can reach heights of four hundred feet. Cedar trail-posts guide hikers across the loose sand to the beach. Besides its well-publicized off-highway vehicle areas, the recreation area rolls out natural beaches and dunes, teeming estuaries, and coastal lakes. Habitats support hummingbirds, deer, frogs, raccoon, and nesting plovers.

Reedsport doubles as the jump-off for Dean Creek Elk Viewing Area. A 3.5-mile detour east on Oregon Highway 38 finds the meadow frequented by sixty to one hundred Roosevelt elk, just one more jewel in the bottomless trove of the Oregon coast.

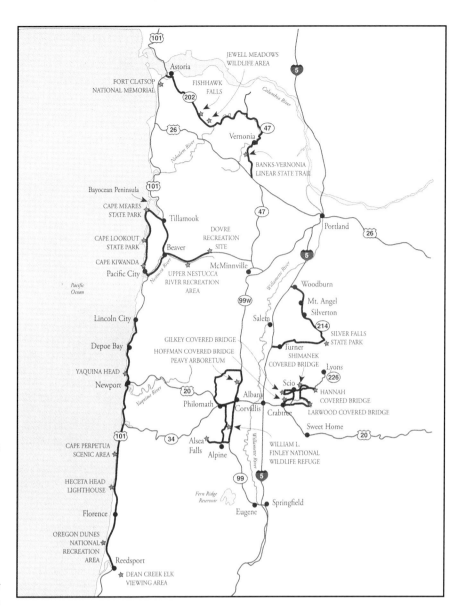

BRIDGES

Architecturally, Oregon's coastal bridges are among the nation's finest, and eligible for listing on the National Register of Historic Places. Many spans on the Pacific Coast Scenic Byway were built in the 1920s and 1930s, the vision of Conde B. McCullough, master bridge builder. His concept of bridge design combined aesthetics with function. Hallmarks of a McCullough bridge include soaring arches, dignified gateway spires, architectural railings, Art Deco pylons, and gothic columns. The results are civil engineering landmarks.

Historic McCullough bridges in Astoria are the Old Youngs Bay Bridge and the Lewis and Clark River Bridge; Tillamook's representative is the Wilson River Bridge. A lineup of these photogenic concrete bridges begins at Depoe Bay and continues south along U.S. 101. Alsea Bay Bridge, the only McCullough bridge to have been replaced (back in 1991), uses original architectural pieces in its design.

By Rhonda and George Osterlag

FROM SISTERS, THIS 82-MILE CIRCUIT LINKS OREGON HIGHWAY 242 (OPEN JULY THROUGH OCTOBER) WITH OREGON HIGHWAY 126 AND U.S. HIGHWAY 20 (BOTH OPEN YEAR-ROUND). OFF U.S. 20 IS FOREST ROAD 14, A MUST-SEE SPUR INTO THE METOLIUS RIVER RECREATION CORRIDOR.

VOLCANO CENTRAL

MCKENZIE PASS TO SANTIAM PASS SCENIC BYWAY

UPPER PROXY FALLS AND ITS COMPANION, LOWER PROXY FALLS, EACH PLUMMET TWO HUNDRED FEET AND ARE EASILY REACHED BY A POPULAR HIKE IN THE THREE SISTERS WILDERNESS. LAVA FLOW AND FOREST SHAPE THE FALLS ENVIRONMENT.

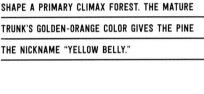

T he adjective for this drive is "spectacular." This central Cascades route showcases stunning volcanoes, two wilderness areas, wild and scenic rivers, some impressive waterfalls, and magnificent Clear Lake. The 75 square miles of lava flows, craters, and cinder cones speak to the area's fiery beginnings. Ponderosa pines, western larches, aspens, and old-growth Douglas firs vary the forest tapestry. The ample trailheads, viewpoints, and campgrounds allow visitors to step into the bounty.

At the junction of U.S. 20 and Oregon Highway 242, on the west side of Sisters, sits the East Portal information wayside—the chosen start. The route begins and ends at Sisters,

a picturesque tourist and agricultural town, with an 1880s western-frontier facade. There, shop windows display western sculpture and art, bright-colored quilts, handcrafted log furniture, and a bonanza of sundries. Creekside Park in Sisters offers picnicking and camping along Whychus Creek.

Llamas share the Three Sisters volcano backdrop as Highway 242 rolls south. The beginning of the route is straightforward, touring areas of ponderosa pine, gradually adding firs and twists with the climb. It then traces the crooked boundary between the Mount Washington and Three Sisters wilderness areas. At the close range afforded by the drive, the volcanic sisterly trio and the pointed helmet of

Mount Washington rise up imposingly. In fall, the red and scarlet leaves of vine maples add touches of color to the sharp, hardened sea of the lava flow.

Dee Wright Observatory, Scott Lake, and Proxy Falls are the most popular stops on Highway 242, but any turnout or trail will satisfy with scenic beauty. The Pacific Crest Trail threads across the forbidding lava near Dee Wright Observatory. This round fortress built of lava seems to have risen from the flow. Its windows of odd shape and size pinpoint the volcanic landmarks. The locator compass on the open roof likewise identifies the neighborhood. In fall, crossbills may flock at the observatory, harvesting seeds from the conifers that surround the lava flow. A paved path travels atop the flow for a closer look at the 1,500-year-old lava. A few silvered snags and tortured trees rise among the appendages of melted rock.

At the base of Scott Mountain, shallow Scott Lake is a favorite for its Three Sisters reflections, quiet lake

SHALLOW SCOTT LAKE SERVES UP BOLD VIEWS OF NORTH AND MIDDLE SISTERS, TWO OF THE THREE
SISTERS. TUCKED BETWEEN THE MOUNT WASHINGTON AND THREE SISTERS WILDERNESS AREAS, THE
LAKE OFFERS PICNICKING AND PRIMITIVE CAMPING, AND SERVES AS A HUB FOR WILDERNESS TRAILS.

THE CHARMING FRONTIER TOWN OF SISTERS IS
KNOWN FOR ITS GALLERIES AND THE SURROUNDING
LLAMA RANCHES.

B&B COMPLEX FIRE

The great lightning fire of 2003—
the B&B Complex Fire—consumed
more than ninety thousand acres in
Deschutes and Willamette National
Forests; evidence of the blaze lingers
along U.S. Highway 20. Although
the fire led to the evacuation of
Camp Sherman, heroic efforts of
firefighters spared the town and
the Metolius Wild and Scenic River
corridor it borders. Normally, the
blackened slopes fulfill nature's
cycle to restore forest health.
The extreme results here are the
outcome of years of fire suppression.
Fire is an agent to good forest health,
scouring out debris, culling trees,
killing insects and disease, opening
seeds, and returning nutrients to
the soil. Fire suppression allows
the fuel base to get out of control,
resulting in hot, fast, sweeping
fires that are more destructive than
beneficial.

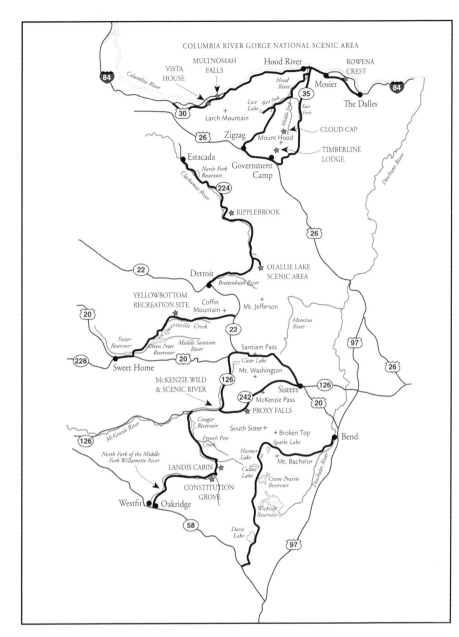

recreation, camping, and network of trails that top Scott Mountain and that visit several lakes. Proxy Falls Trail visits a pair of waterfalls showing nature's sleight-of-hand. In this ultimate bottomless-glass trick, the 200-foot cascading waterfalls plummet to dead-end pools that never overflow. (I could tell readers that the explanation rests with the porous lava, but I believe the illusion is more fun.)

Where the loop follows Highway 126, travelers enter the house of Clear Lake and the McKenzie Wild and Scenic River, and boy, what a house! Here, big Douglas firs and hemlocks shape a strong visual aisle. Clear Lake, created by a lava blockage and fed by Great Spring, is the dazzling, chilly (too

cold for swimming) lake at the river's headwater. Remnants of the forest that drowned 3,000 years ago remain preserved one hundred feet underwater. A picturesque forest-and-flow setting encompasses the lake. A trail around the lake shows off the place, its ospreys, and mergansers.

The lake's west shore holds two popular rustic attractions, a USFS picnic area and a Linn County Parks resort. Besides offering fine lake views, the resort rents rowboats and cabins, and during summer, its small restaurant serves breakfast and lunch.

The acclaimed McKenzie River unfurls in spectacular dark pools, blue-ice cascades, bubbling eddies, and two major waterfalls: 63-foot Koosah

(reached at Ice Cap Campground) and 100-foot Sahalie (0.2 mile to its north). Both falls areas can be reached by driving, but hikers and mountain bikers may prefer taking the McKenzie River National Recreation Trail, a 26-mile trail that pursues the river downstream from its origin to the community of McKenzie Bridge (a second byway portal). A favorite hiking loop travels the national recreation trail and Falls Trail to encircle the waterfall duo, passing between the upper bridge and Carmen Reservoir. Numerous cascades add to the viewing excitement.

U.S. 20 likewise presents a spectacular setting but at a whisked pace. Here, Black Butte and Mount Jefferson are the skyline royalty. Side trips to such places as the Hoodoo Ski area/Big Lake area, Suttle Lake, and Black Butte, and access to luxury resorts and campgrounds can side-track travelers.

A trip into the Camp Sherman–Metolius River area slows the pace and treats eyes to a breathtaking spring-fed river. The Metolius Wild and Scenic River captivates with its deep trenches, riffles, and pools, and its ponderosa pine–western larch setting. Cedars grow riverside and grassy bars and islands flaunt big-leaf lupine, Indian paintbrush, and monkeyflower. This river secludes large wild trout and its fly-fishing sport is world-renowned. USFS campgrounds dot the recreation corridor, along with private campgrounds and resorts. Key attractions include the Head of the Metolius, the Camp Sherman fish-viewing platform, and Wizard Falls Fish Hatchery. Foot trails trace the river's banks.

By Rhonda and George Osterlag

FIRE
and FEATHERS

VOLCANO SCENIC BYWAY
TO CRATER LAKE AND
KLAMATH BASIN

THIS 140-MILE BYWAY BEGINS AT DIAMOND LAKE JUNCTION, THE INTERCEPTION OF U.S. HIGHWAY 97 AND OREGON HIGHWAY 138 (10 MILES SOUTH OF CHEMULT). IT FOLLOWS OREGON HIGHWAY 138, CRATER LAKE NORTH ENTRANCE ROAD (CLOSED IN WINTER), RIM DRIVE, OREGON HIGHWAY 62, WEED ROAD, SEVENMILE ROAD, WESTSIDE ROAD, AND OREGON HIGHWAY 140 TO U.S. 97 SOUTH, BEFORE ENDING AT THE CALIFORNIA BORDER.

AT A DEPTH OF 1,958 FEET, CRATER LAKE IS THE SECOND DEEPEST NATURAL LAKE IN THE WESTERN HEMISPHERE AND THE SEVENTH DEEPEST IN THE WORLD. IT RESIDES IN OREGON'S ONLY NATIONAL PARK.

his drive through the southern Cascades and Klamath Basin is a journey of fire and feathers. The route crosses ashy pine forest and climbs to encircle the caldera rim of the miraculously blue Crater Lake, before descending into the mosaic of forest, range, lake, and wetland that makes up Klamath Basin. Skyline views include Mount Thielsen, the remnant volcanic cones of ancient Mount Mazama, the caldera of Mountain Lakes Wilderness, and California's Mount Shasta. A pumice desert, fumaroles (the welded spires around vents of escaping gas), and cinder cones continue the fiery tale.

Klamath Basin hosts 80 percent of the migratory birds on the Pacific Flyway. Millions of waterfowl arrive in the fall, with an entourage of bald eagles.

The legacy from Mount Mazama's eruption and collapse precedes the turnoff to Crater Lake National Park. The nutrient-lacking ashy and pumiceous soils sustain only the hardiest of trees—the lodgepole pine. As the route climbs, the forest fills out, adding other species. Side roads beckon detours to trailheads and other attractions.

The route then arrives at Crater Lake National Park via the north entrance. At the caldera, it adds a circle, following

the 33-mile Rim Drive, which serves up multiple overlooks of the 5-mile-wide, 1,900-foot-deep lake. The sky and the steep-sided golden cliffs of the caldera are reflected in the mesmerizing lake. Piercing the lake, the volcanic cone of Wizard Island rises seven hundred feet above the surface. The small, aptly named jagged-top island, Phantom Ship, cuts an eerie profile. Place-names such as Devils Backbone, Pumice Castle, Danger Bay, and Sun Notch spark imagination. Several turnouts have panels explaining the area's geology and relating the associated Native American legends.

Rim Drive also leads to trails. Paths strike up Watchman Peak and Mount Scott (both of which hold lookouts) or descend to Cleetwood Cove, which is the launch site for the park's boat tour and the sole lake access. The boat tour is a fee attraction. At Rim Village, visitors find the historic Crater Lake Lodge (built in 1915 and completely restored), Sinnott Memorial Observation Station, and the trail to Garfield Peak (elevation 8,060 feet). Many hikers consider Garfield Peak to have the finest summit view in the park. The village attends to needs with food services, a picnic area, and a small visitor center.

Travelers may opt for a detour off Rim Drive to the Pinnacles. This 6-mile detour finds an impressive canyon array of fumaroles (peculiar spire-shaped vents). Trails wander the rim of the narrow canyon, offering changing perspectives. Along one trail, visitors may find the abandoned East Entrance. Where the primary drive leaves the park, the Godfrey Glen and Annie Falls areas offer a second opportunity to see similar geologic features.

The park averages 44 feet of snow per year, and the white stuff can linger into July. Wildflowers have a brief season; their fragile blooms pierce the ash and pumice, top mountains, and grace creeks and waterfalls. Sightings of big wildlife are rare, but the Clark's nutcrackers, ground squirrels, and chipmunks are entertaining. Additional park overlooks and picnic areas, as well as the park's Mazama Campground, line the route south.

History flavors the journey at the hamlet of Fort Klamath. The frontier fort here garrisoned the Oregon Volunteer Cavalry between 1863 and 1890. And here, the trial and execution of Captain Jack marked the final chapter in the Modoc Indian Wars (1872–1873). The military had been ordered to round up the Modocs and place them on a reservation with the Klamath Indians— their historic enemy. But under Captain Jack, a ragtag band of fifty-two Modocs held off cavalry troops, who were superior in number, for five months in the harsh lava lands of what is now Lava

WIZARD ISLAND IS ONE OF TWO CINDER CONES IN CRATER LAKE; THE OTHER IS SUBMERGED. THE LAKE'S INTENSE BLUE COLOR TAKES ON DIFFERENT HUES WITH THE SEASON AND ANGLE OF SUNLIGHT.

YELLOW-HEADED BLACKBIRDS FREQUENT THE MANY MARSHLANDS OF THE KLAMATH BASIN.

Beds National Monument in northern California. Surrender, though, was inevitable. Newspaper reports of the standoff fanned the attention of the nation.

Today at the fort, simple white markers identify the graves of Captain Jack and three other Modoc leaders. Although a gopher-started fire swept much of the Fort Klamath Historic Site Museum, the graves were spared, along with a jail and an old post office. A re-created guardhouse now holds the replacement museum.

After Fort Klamath, the route takes a couple of jigs to travel the western outskirts of the Upper Klamath Basin. Pastures, barbed wire, rustic corrals, distant farmhouses, aspens, cattails, and forested slopes paint the backdrop. Signs announce side routes to trails entering the Sky Lakes and Mountain Lakes wildernesses.

By Crystal Springs Picnic Area, the route edges Upper Klamath National Wildlife Refuge and its 90,000-acre lake. Boat launches at Malone Springs and Rocky Point offer easy access to the 9.5-mile Upper Klamath Canoe Trail. Rocky Point Resort rents canoes. The quiet paddle reveals marsh, open water, and forests and offers chance encounters with beaver, geese, swans,

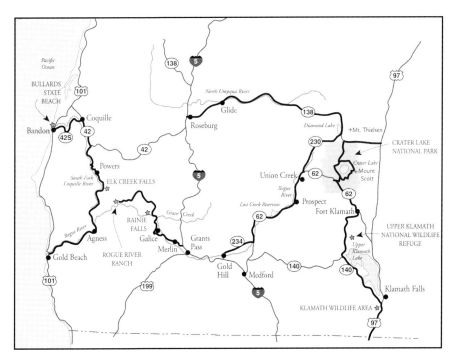

and other wildlife. Primitive Odessa Creek Campground, off OR 140, signals another chance to slide the canoe into refuge waters.

The drive now rolls over low forested hills and dips back into the basin. From turnouts, travelers can view western grebes, herons, ducks, and terns. The view at Howard Bay provides the first sense of the enormity of Upper Klamath Lake.

Where U.S. 97 makes its quick run to the Oregon-California border, travelers

can detour west on Miller Island Road to Klamath Wildlife Area for birding. In spring, sandhill cranes can be seen with their young, and white pelicans adorn the sky. Owls favor the big shade trees near the old farm. Views stretch across the marsh to Mount Shasta.

Reaching the border, travelers may choose to end the drive, or follow U.S. 97 into California to Lower Klamath National Wildlife Refuge (more feathers).

By Rhonda and George Osterlag

THIS 190-MILE CRESCENT OFF
INTERSTATE 84 SWEEPS EAST FROM
LA GRANDE (EXIT 261) ON OREGON
HIGHWAY 82 TO JOSEPH, WHERE IT
FOLLOWS OREGON HIGHWAY 350,
FOREST ROAD 39, AND OREGON
HIGHWAY 86, RETURNING TO
INTERSTATE 84 AT EXIT 302, JUST
NORTH OF BAKER CITY. WINTER SNOW
CLOSES FOREST ROAD 39.

PARADISE FOUND

HELLS CANYON SCENIC BYWAY MAIN LOOP

THE IMNAHA WILD AND SCENIC RIVER WORKS ITS
WAY THROUGH THE STEEP, ARID STEPPES OF HELLS
CANYON NATIONAL RECREATION AREA.

This backroad revels in spectacle. It travels the ranchland of the Grande Ronde and Wallowa river valleys, passes around and through the Wallowa high-mountain grandeur, overlooks the stunning, harsh wild of Hells Canyon, and traverses Pine Creek Valley to meet up with the Oregon Trail at Flagstaff Hill. Welcoming small towns, the bronze art at Joseph, or a live production at the Elgin Opera House, opened in 1912, can waylay travelers. The heritage of the Nez Perce Indians lives on in the landmarks, the celebrations, and the spirit of the land.

For outdoor recreation, the region teems with opportunities: camping, hiking, horseback riding, rafting, and fishing. For trail information and passes, three USFS offices in La Grande, Joseph, and Halfway serve the area. Private horse- and llama-packers lead trips into the deeper wilds of Eagle Cap Wilderness (the heart of the Wallowas) and Hells Canyon. For a top of the mountain perspective, the four-passenger gondola lift of Wallowa Lake Tram ascends 3,200 vertical feet to the summit of Mount Howard, at 8,256 feet. Byway spurs can extend the road trip to Imnaha, notably wild and remote, and to

the Snake River at Copperfield, once the site of a riotous mining town. In these lonesome parts, self-reliance is key.

Broad agricultural flats in the Grande Ronde Valley stretch to folded savannah ridges, before giving way to more rolling terrain. Irrigation lines, railroad tracks, and farmhouses buried in cottonwood stands all contribute to views. Small towns tout their local teams, while the rustic screen doors of quaint general stores beg to be opened.

From Minam Hill, travelers descend into a dramatic canyon of basalt-terraced rims, heading for the Minam and Wallowa rivers. Past the Minam State Park turnoff, the satiny liquid band of the Wallowa River pairs with the byway. Where the valley broadens, travelers' pulses may be elevated by early views of the "Little Switzerland of North America"—the Wallowa Mountains.

Wallowa, Lostine, Enterprise, and Joseph serve as northern gateways to the Wallowas. The surrounding ranchland clears the way to grand mountain panoramas. Eagle Cap Wilderness encompasses 361,000 acres of these prized mountains, including more than fifty named peaks. The Matterhorn, the tallest, tops out at 9,845 feet. Crystalline rivers, high lakes, hanging valleys, ice fields, steeple-topped conifers, and alpine meadows seal the invitation.

The small town of Joseph has shaken off its dusty frontier image, finding bronze. Along the cobblestone walks of Main Street, more than a dozen major life-like bronze sculptures glint under the mountain sun. Among the subjects are wild animals, Nez Perce Indians, cowboys, horses, and a barefoot girl on a garden walk.

THE ENTIRE LENGTH OF THE IMNAHA RIVER IS DESIGNATED A WILD AND SCENIC RIVER. IT JOURNEYS FROM THE HIGH WALLOWA MOUNTAINS THROUGH FOREST AND DESERT CANYON BEFORE IT EMPTIES INTO THE SNAKE RIVER.

The inspirational Wallowa Mountains setting is perfect for artists and for foundries and galleries of all art forms to flourish. To the casual observer, it seems natural for the store fronts of art to intermingle with the shops of western sundries. Both Joseph and Enterprise, have earned places on the Americans for the Arts list of "100 Best Small Art Towns in America."

At the head of the valley sits gorgeous Wallowa Lake, with its extensive state park and wilderness trails that follow the forks of the Wallowa River into the high country. The lake cupped by high peaks and contained by a glacial moraine shimmers a stunning blue and has a full line-up of recreational pursuits, with swimming, fishing, boating, and parasailing. Chief Joseph's grave sits at the lake's foot.

The byway then leaves Joseph following Highway 350 toward Imnaha, rounding the Wallowa Mountain centerpiece. Ranchland, beautiful barns, and mountain views precede the right turn onto Wallowa Mountain Road/ Forest Road 39. The route straight ahead is the untaken Imnaha spur.

Wallowa Mountain Road twists out of the Little Sheep Creek drainage for an ear-popping ascent to Salt Spring Summit. In places, snag forests left by the Canal Fire of 1989 give the mountains a hoary stubble. Deer and elk can surprise travelers. The route passes from Wallowa-Whitman National Forest into Hells Canyon National Recreation Area. Past the Imnaha River recreation sites, where the route again climbs, a left turn on Forest Road 3965 travels 3 miles (4.8 km) to Hells Canyon Overlook. Here, visitors find a paved walk, benches, interpretive panels, loads of wildflowers, and inspiring views on the canyon brink. An impressive 1.5 miles (2.4km) deep with an average width of 10 miles (16.1 km), Hells Canyon reigns as the deepest gorge in North America. Idaho's Seven Devils add a bold skyline to the humbling drop.

The Pine Creek drainage then leads travelers out of the mountains and across the valley. Where Forest Road 39 meets Highway 86, a detour east leads to the Snake River at Copperfield, where camping is available. The primary driving route follows Highway 86 west through Halfway and Richland, southern gateways to the Wallowa Mountains and the mountain line-up of recreation. Richland also provides access to Brownlee Reservoir on the Powder River. Views sweep across the rolling ranchland and rangeland at the foot of the Wallowas and stretch west up the Powder River drainage to the Elkhorns.

At Flagstaff Hill, the National Historic Oregon Trail Interpretive Center has a fine museum, trails, the Meeker Monument, wagon encampment interpretive program, and views of original trail ruts. Summer walks on the sun-baked trails give visitors a tiny taste of the pioneer experience. As the byway hurries toward Interstate 84, it passes the obelisk commemorating the centennial of the Oregon Trail. From 1843 to 1869, some 250,000 pioneers braved the arduous trek.

At Interstate 84, Baker City sits 2 miles (3.2 km) south; it's 41 miles (66 km) north to close the loop at La Grande.

A STREET-SIDE COLLECTION OF LIFE-SIZE BRONZE STATUES, INCLUDING THIS SOARING EAGLE, IS THE HALLMARK OF JOSEPH, A TOWN WHICH SUCCESSFULLY BLENDS COWBOY BOOTS AND ART.

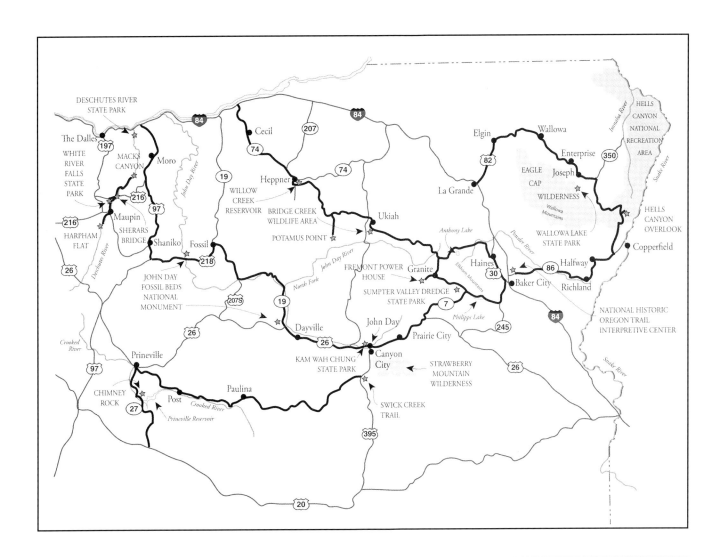

CHIEF JOSEPH AND THE NEZ PERCE

The Wallowa Valley was the traditional home of the usually peaceful Nez Perce (a.k.a. Nee-Mee-Poo) Indians. But the year 1877 changed all that, when trouble arising from the increase in white settlement led to a call for the U.S. military to evict the tribe from the valley. That order sent young Chief Joseph and the men, women, and children of his tribe on a 1,700-mile freedom quest to Canada. The path included a dangerous crossing of the unfettered Snake River in Hells Canyon during high water. Women, children, the sick, and the elderly road atop horsehide rafts pulled by riders on swimming horses. The tribe brought with them thousands of horses and cows. While great numbers of livestock drowned, no tribe member was lost. Chief Joseph nearly succeeded in gaining freedom for his people; he was captured just 40 miles (64.4 km) from the Canadian border at Bear Paw, Montana. Although the descendants of the tribe are now dispersed, the Wallowas hold their cultural heart.

The town of Joseph, established in 1887, wears the name of young Chief Joseph, and two of the nearby peaks, Chief Joseph Mountain and Mount Howard, recall this page in history. The latter was named for the Army officer in charge of the eviction.

Each July since 1945, the town of Joseph has celebrated Chief Joseph Days, a tribute to the Nez Perce leader and the Old West. The tribal homecoming celebration, Tamkaliks, also in July, features a powwow and the Homecoming Dance in full regalia. Small tribal museums in both Joseph and Wallowa preserve the Indian perspective.

The chief's father, old Chief Joseph, now rests at the foot of Wallowa Lake; his remains were relocated here in 1925, after his original grave had been raided. At the site, spiritual trinkets and mementos—feathers, beads, grass bundles, wood carvings, tobacco, bandannas, and dream catchers—honor the chief.

Chapter 7

WASHINGTON

CARBON RIVER VALLEY IN

MOUNT RAINIER NATIONAL

PARK, WASHINGTON.

JAMES MARVIN PHELPS/

SHUTTERSTOCK

By Diana Fairbanks and Mike Sedam

FROM LA PUSH, TRAVEL EAST ON WASHINGTON HIGHWAY 110 TOWARD FORKS. THERE, TURN RIGHT ON U.S. HIGHWAY 101 AND FOLLOW IT SOUTH TO QUEETS, THEN FOLLOW THE HIGHWAY SOUTHEAST TOWARD LAKE QUINAULT. AT THE SOUTH END OF THE LAKE, FOLLOW U.S. 101 TO HOQUIAM AND ABERDEEN.

WILD BEACHES

LA PUSH TO HOQUIAM

COMMERCIAL FISHING BOATS MOOR IN FRONT OF
A DRY DOCK IN A RIVER NEAR HOQUIAM.
MIKE SEDAM

This backroad has rich possibilities on either side. The east side features the interior rainforest flanking the Olympic Mountains. This adventure will emphasize the wondrous coastal beaches on the west side of U.S. 101.

Geologically, the Olympic Peninsula is merely twelve million years or so old, making it a relatively late add-on to the continent of North America. Those who travel this byway glory in the annex and all its features. Rain forests, mountains, fertile rivers, timber, beaches, and quiet trails are all available to adventurers.

The start of this byway is La Push, a small oceanfront town that has been occupied by the Quileute tribe. Try to visit both sides of the Quillayute River. The La Push Road (Highway 101) goes to First Beach, Second Beach, and Third Beach on the south side of the river. Turn onto Mora Road to get to Rialto Beach. Anticipate some short hikes at the end of the road to reach the waterline; these are well worth the trouble. Bring a picnic and a camera.

In Forks, head south on US. 101. The highway eventually turns toward the coast, following the Hoh River to the sea. It pops out of the forest and follows the Pacific Ocean at Ruby Beach and the Hoh Indian Reservation.

This roadway from Ruby Beach to the town of Queets is a summer treat and a winter storm watcher's secret. The road twists and turns, encountering cliffs and deep forests and surprising ocean views. Beaches 6, 5, 4, 3, 2, 1, South Beach, and the Kalaloch Rocks stop cars, especially on the rare clear, warm summer day. Most stops involve parking the car and hiking through coastal forests to the beach below. Drop by Kalaloch for its information station. Compared to

THIS VIEW OF SPLIT ROCK IS TYPICAL OF THE FORMATIONS AND BEACH ACCESS WEST OF FORKS ON WASHINGTON HIGHWAY 110. *MIKE SEDAM*

mountain rain forests, coastal beach forests are dense but neatly clipped by wind and driven rain.

The Quinault Indian Reservation at Queets marks a turn away from the coast for U.S. 101. It follows the Salmon River Valley to beautiful Lake Quinault. The lake, which can be circuited by North and South Shore Roads, has two ranger stations and another rain forest access on its north side. July Falls Creek State Parks offer camping and elk. Some services are available at Amanda Park and Quinault. Easy hiking trails surround the grand old Lake Quinault Lodge, which proudly serves up fine accommodations for those who don't care to rough it at the beach.

From Quinault, U.S. 101 heads south toward Aberdeen and Hoquiam, the towns that lumber built. Halfway there, you'll arrive at a town whose name causes much merriment: Humptulips. A turnoff takes you to the seaside towns of Pacific Beach, Copalis Beach, and Ocean City.

Hoquiam has a proud logging tradition and many examples of the machines and history that marked its early days. Log shipping still generates the dollars here. But its location on Gray's Harbor also make it the closest large city to the resort area of Ocean Shores and the state park at Ocean City. All kinds of services and supplies are available.

Washington residents have spent many shining happy moments on these Pacific beaches with families on summer trips. The deep dense forests and wide sand stretches still have a kind of magic. They beg for running with kites, poking in driftwood, looking up at canopies of green, watching animals, getting muddy, cooling off, eating around campfires, and thinking of the world as a big amazing planet. Experience them for yourself and feel like a kid again.

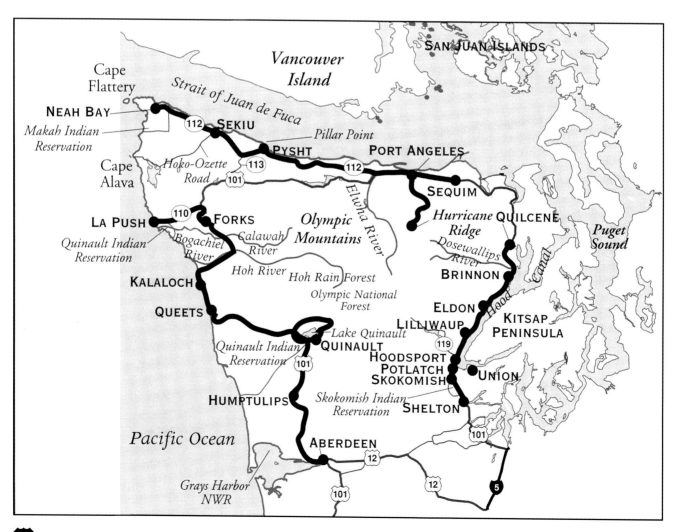

By Diana Fairbanks and Mike Sedam

BEGIN IN BUCKLEY ON WASHINGTON HIGHWAY 410. DRIVE SOUTHWEST AND TAKE A LEFT TURN ONTO HIGHWAY 165, HEADING SOUTH TO WILKESON. AFTER CARBONADO, THE HIGHWAY SPLITS. TAKE THE FORK TO THE RIGHT AND ENTER MOUNT RAINIER NATIONAL PARK. THE ROAD ENDS AT A CAMPSITE ALONGSIDE MOWICH LAKE.

CARBONADO

BUCKLEY TO MOWICH LAKE

THIS STEEL ARCH, AN EXAMPLE OF ENGINEERING ELEGANCE, SPANS A DEEP GREEN CANYON ON WASHINGTON HIGHWAY 165 AS IT APPROACHED THE BOUNDARY OF MOUNT RAINIER NATIONAL PARK.

MIKE SEDAM

FALSE-FRONT ARCHITECTURE, TYPICAL OF BOOMTOWN DAYS WHEN COAL MINING WAS HIGHLY PROFITABLE, DISTINGUISHES THESE OLD STORES ON WASHINGTON HIGHWAY 165. *MIKE SEDAM*

In the late 1800s, when settlers began occupying the western territories, natural resources seemed to have infinite profit potential. Fuel for progress, in the form of coal deposits, occurs in abundance in western Washington; people such as Samuel Wilkeson, Jr., invested in coal mining and transportation empires and created boomtowns in the process. Other towns exploited their timber resources with similar results.

This backroad travels through some of those former boomtowns on the way to a more contemporary asset, a rustic recreational site and staging area for mountain appreciation of all kinds.

A town of forty-three hundred, Buckley is a timber settlement at the edge of the city sprawl around Puget Sound. Its annual Loggers Rodeo celebrates skills formerly needed to work here. Logging trucks still rumble along Highway 410, carrying harvests from the Cascade Mountains. However, Buckley has evolved to offer recreation equipment rentals and services as well. Drive south through town to the junction with Washington Highway 165 (look for signs to Wilkeson). On the way to Wilkeson, pass the grocery store that is in the town of Burnett.

Wilkeson was founded in 1880 and in only twenty years boasted a growing population of coal miners and their families. It was named for Samuel Wilkeson, Jr., the corporate board secretary of the Northern Pacific Railroad and prime investor in the Wilkeson Coal and Coke Company. The town was named for him as a present for his sixtieth birthday. He shipped coal, via the railroad, to supply iron refineries in Tacoma. Remnants of "uptown" Wilkeson, rows of identical company houses, still survive, as does a school built in 1913 and the oldest Orthodox Church in the lower forty-eight states.

Today, travelers purchase gas, water, and food in Wilkeson, since none are available at Mowich Lake. The Mount Rainier National Park Wilderness Information Center in town issues permits for park uses and answers questions.

Drive south on Highway 165 past Carbonado, another town with a coal surge in its history. In the 1930s, oil became the fuel of choice for transportation and lighting and coal mining dwindled. Facing expensive safety requirements, Carbonado mines closed in 1974, with 98% of their deposits untapped. Now the town is a gateway to the national park, as well as the Mt. Baker-Snoqualmie National Forest and Clearwater Wilderness Area.

Out of Carbonado, the highway crosses a one-lane iron bridge over a deep rock canyon, with the Carbon River far below. Less than a mile from the bridge, you have two options. You can take the left fork in the road to reach the Carbon River entrance of the national park and the popular Ipsut Creek Campground. Since the access road to the campground seems to be in the bed of Ipsut Creek, expect some bumpy going. Or you can turn right at the fork, climbing on unpaved roadway, passing the Evans Creek ORV area and arriving at the Mowich Lake park entrance. A self-pay station collects fees from those who did not buy passes at Wilkeson.

Mount Rainier National Park protects mountainsides of lush green old-growth. On this route, private companies log areas just outside the park boundaries. The contrasts are dramatic, although the scraped hillsides do afford big views of the Carbon River Valley.

End your road trip at the parking lot for the Mowich Lake walk-in campground. No reservations are offered, and this primitive campground (chemical toilets and no water) is fully occupied on some sunny summer weekends. It is a stopover for hikers taking the Wonderland Trail, which winds around the entire mountain, as well as a starting point for numerous other popular trails within the park.

Mowich Lake itself is a beautiful sub-alpine waterway pocketed under Mother Mountain and Elizabeth Ridge. Its meadows burst with wildflowers after snowmelt. A small ranger's cabin shelters summer naturalists and rangers. It's safe to say a lot of cameras have clicked at this lake.

MOWICH LAKE IS A BEAUTIFUL SUB-ALPINE WATERWAY POCKETED UNDER MOTHER MOUNTAIN AND ELIZABETH RIDGE. IT'S SAFE TO SAY A LOT OF CAMERAS HAVE CLICKED AT THIS LAKE.
KYPHUA/SHUTTERSTOCK

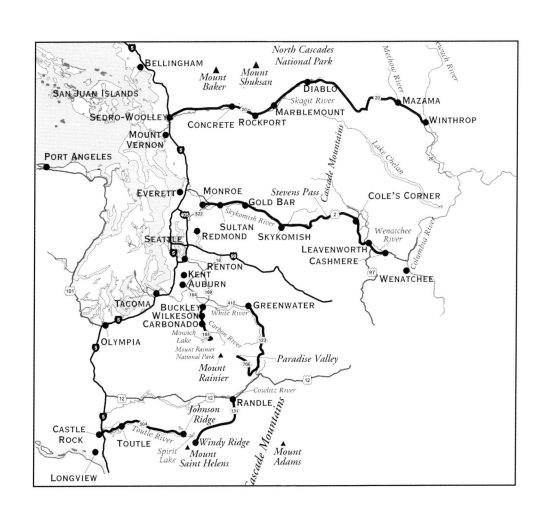

By Diana Fairbanks and Mike Sedam

FROM PALOUSE, DRIVE NORTH ON WASHINGTON HIGHWAY 27, PASSING THROUGH GARFIELD, BELMONT, AND OAKESDALE. IN OAKESDALE, TURN LEFT ONTO HUME ROAD, FOLLOWING SIGNS TO STEPTOE BUTTE STATE PARK. AT THE PARK ENTRANCE, TURN RIGHT AND FOLLOW THE ROAD TO THE SUMMIT OF THE BUTTE.

STEPTOE

PALOUSE TO STEPTOE BUTTE

FRESHLY BALED HAY SOAKS UP A LITTLE MORE
SUMMER SUN ON A HILLSIDE NEAR FARMINGTON.
MIKE SEDAM

IRRIGATION VIA THE COLUMBIA RIVER RECLAMATION
PROJECT MADE THE ARID PLATEAUS OF EASTERN
WASHINGTON BURST WITH AGRICULTURAL
POSSIBILITIES. *MIKE SEDAM*

The little town of Palouse now finds itself on a Washington State Scenic Byway. Seems travelers from Spokane and even the Puget Sound cities have warmed to the sweet rural delights of this wheat-growing region. Although Steptoe Butte is the significant destination for this byway, weathered barns, antique farm equipment, and farmhouses nestled in groves of trees along the route inspire photographs and nostalgia.

Palouse sits on the river of the same name in a region that was populated by the Palouse tribe. They were noted for their horsemanship and a unique breed of horses with dappled fur. The breed is now called Appaloosa, a contraction of "a Palouse's" horse.

Drive north from Palouse on Washington Highway 27 through endless rolling hills planted with wheat or pasturing beef cattle. Photographers seek vignettes of weathered farm life here like miners pan for gold. Courteous visitors observe some rules: First, ask for permission to enter private lands; second, leave everything exactly as it was, including pasture gates, and third, be sensitive to fire danger in dry grasslands.

The highway passes Garfield, which has a population of 618, a quiet city park, and beautiful old homes. Next is Belmont, which consists of a grain elevator. Oakesdale is 22 miles (35.4 km) from Palouse, but these are country miles, made to be taken slowly and without cellular phones. Oakesdale has a population of 441 with some of its citizens residing in homes on the National Historic Register. Pick up bottled water or other beverages here.

Turn left onto Hume Road, following signs to the state park. It's almost 8 miles (12.9 km) from the turn to the butte itself, and this country road continues in dry land farm territory. All the while, the butte gets closer and bigger.

Geologically, Steptoe Butte is a formation of pink quartzite. It is a remnant of a shoreline from the young North American continent, pushed inland by a plateau of lava flows, which were scoured to their basalt core by epochal flooding at the end of the last ice age. Historically, it's a prominent landmark believed to facilitate vision quests by tribes of the region. Later, it was the site of military reconnaissance, and, even later, a grand hotel built by an eccentric entrepreneur. Now it's the apex of a 150-acre state park with a view unequaled.

At the entrance to the park, turn right to begin the spiral up the butte. Though it's less than 4 miles (6.4 km) from the turnoff to the summit, this part of the drive seems to take a long time. Maybe that's because there is so much to look at on the way up. Stands of ponderosa pine, Douglas fir, and apple trees near the base give way to open grassy hillsides toward the top. The park harbors deer, elk, coyote, and rabbits. Hawks use the upper reaches of the butte for launching food searches, while pheasant and quail seek the grasslands and tree cover.

At the top, very few amenities impede the view. With good weather, it is possible to see the Cascade Mountains over 120 miles (193.1 km) to the west, as well as the Blue Mountains to the south. The farmland at the base of the butte is laid out in squares with roads binding them together. Park in an ample lot and take a short walk to picnic tables and barbeques. Toilets are available but water is not. Some motorists bring bicycles and coast back down the hill.

Geologists now speak of structures like this one as a "steptoe" formation, but the butte was named for Colonel Edward Steptoe, a cavalry commander charged with keeping peace in times when tribes were being forced to move to reservations. He used the butte to scout the movements of the Spokane and Nez Perce tribes and locate new farms and settlements. His career is remembered for a failed attempt to force Spokane Indians to leave settlement lands near Rosalia.

Local tribes called the butte "Eomoshtoss" or Power Mountain.

They went to the mountain on personal vision quests to seek their totems and strengths.

The colorful "Cash-Up" Davis is another visionary in the butte's recorded history. He built a bustling business with a hotel on his homestead below and dreamed of multiplying his fortune by opening a luxury inn on top of the butte – an inn boasting modern amenities and even an observatory with a telescope. He built his dream hotel in 1888, and it did generate a lot of business at first. But after people had been up to see the place, they didn't come back for repeat visits. The hotel was little used when it burned down in 1908.

Steptoe Butte has hosted a lot of dreams. Maybe dreaming is easier with vistas so vast.

FALL WHEAT FIELDS SURROUND CLASSIC FARM
BUILDINGS IN THE FARMING COUNTRY NEAR
PALOUSE. *BOB POOL/SHUTTERSTOCK*

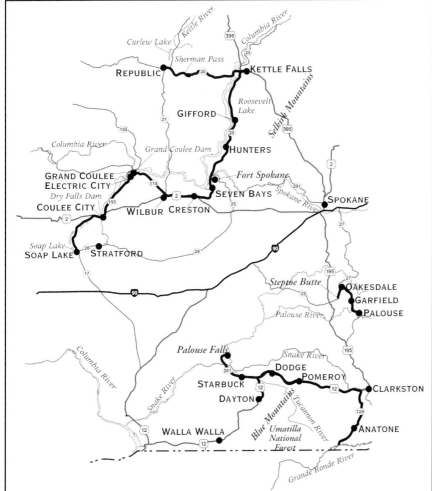

The CONTRIBUTORS

Gary Crabbe is the owner of Enlightened Images Photography (www.enlightphoto.com) and the photographer of Quarto Publishing's Our *San Francisco, Backroads of the California Wine Country,* and *Backroads of the California Coast.*

Diana Fairbanks is an artist, teacher, and author who works from her studio in Olympia, Washington. She has lived in the state for her entire life and enjoys traveling to see its wonders. She is currently completing her "Rivers of Washington Project"—a series of paintings of the waterways throughout the state.

After trying his hand at truck driving, mining, ranching, and a variety of other endeavors, *Jim Hinckley* turned to writing a weekly column on automotive history for his local newspaper, the *Kingman Daily Miner,* in his adopted hometown of Kingman, Arizona. Hinckley has since written extensively on his two primary passions: automotive history and travel. He is the author of *Ghost Towns of Route 66* and *Backroads of Arizona,* and a regular contributor to *Route 66, American Road, Hemmings Classic Car,* and *Old Cars Weekly.* Book reviews and original features on automotive history and travel can be found on his blog at www.jimhinckleysamerica.com and on his popular podcast, *Jim Hinckley's America & Route 66 Adventures.*

Theresa Husarik is a writer, photographer, and Utah resident with a love of travel and the outdoors. Having spent nearly 20 years combing the nooks and crannies of Utah searching for the perfect photo spot, she has discovered many of the joys of traveling the backroads. Her images and articles have appeared in numerous publications worldwide.

For the past thirty years, *Rhonda and George Osterlag* have been uncovering Oregon's prized natural haunts. A half-dozen of the duo's twenty outdoor guide and photography books feature Oregon. Oregon is also well celebrated in their articles, calendars, and postcards. Titles by the couple include *Our Oregon* (Voyageur Press), *Camping Oregon* (a Globe-Pequot FalconGuide), and *Best Short Hikes in Northwest Oregon* and *100 Hikes in Oregon* (The Mountaineers Books). They do slip away from time to time, as seen by their other titles: *Our Washington* (Voyageur Press), *California State Parks: A Complete Recreation Guide* (The Mountaineers Books), and *Hiking New York, Hiking Connecticut and Rhode Island, Hiking Pennsylvania,* and *Scenic Driving Pennsylvania.*

DAVID M. WYMAN

An award-winning guidebook author and travel journalist, *Karen Misuraca* drives, bikes, and hikes the byways and trails of the California coast and wine country, where she lives. Karen is the founder of the online magazine, DeepCultureTravel.com.

Mike Sedam has a primary interest in landscapes honed by over fifty years of freelance travel photography. Mike has seen some of the most beautiful panoramas in the world and learned to elicit strong pictorial composition from them as well as masterful color. He practiced this approach almost weekly on his beloved Mt. Rainier—a landmark that was only minutes from his home. He now is starting new projects in his new home in Cape Coral, Florida.

Claude Wiatrowski has been writing and providing photos for books on Colorado history for more than 30 years. His published works include Railroads of Colorado, *Railroads Across North America, The Cripple Creek & Victor Book,* and *Teller County Colorado.* In addition to writing books, Wiatrowski produces videos on historic railroads. His productions have won Telly and Teddy awards, and one was selected for the Library of Congress Local Legacies Program..

Having picked up photography as a youngster, *David Wyman* has directed a travel and photography program for the University of Southern California, taught nature photography for the UCLA extension program, and conducted photography tours on behalf of Yosemite, the Los Angeles Zoo, and natural history museums. He currently conducts tours for his company, Image Quest Photography. His articles have appeared in *Outdoor Photography, Outside, Sierra, Cross-Country Ski, Sky and Telescope,* and *Westways.*

INDEX

©2021 Quarto Publishing Group USA Inc.

First Published in 2021 by Motorbooks, an imprint of The Quarto Group, 100 Cummings Center, Suite 265-D, Beverly, MA 01915, USA.
T (978) 282-9590 F (978) 283-2742
QuartoKnows.com

Every effort has been made to ensure that credits accurately comply with information supplied. We apologize for any inaccuracies that may have occurred and will resolve inaccurate or missing information in a subsequent reprinting of the book.

Motorbooks titles are also available at discount for retail, wholesale, promotional, and bulk purchase. For details, contact the Special Sales Manager by email at specialsales@quarto.com or by mail at The Quarto Group, Attn: Special Sales Manager, 100 Cummings Center, Suite 265-D, Beverly, MA 01915, USA.

25 24 23 22 21   1 2 3 4 5

ISBN: 978-0-7603-6997-5

Digital edition published in 2021

The content in this book previously appeared in the following Motorbooks titles: *Backroads of Northern California* (2000), *Backroads of Washington* (2004), *Backroads of Oregon* (2005), *Backroads of Southern California* (2005), *Backroads of the California Wine Country* (2006), *Backroads of Arizona, 2nd Edition* (2006), *Route 66 Backroads* (2008), *Backroads of Utah* (2008), *Backroads of the California Coast* (2009), and *Historic Colorado* (2009).

Library of Congress Cataloging-in-Publication Data available.

Design and layout: Burge Agency

Cover image: corumov/Shutterstock; Back cover images: David M. Wyman (top); George Ostertag (bottom)

Photography: Noted with photos; except page 2 Sneaky Buddy/Shutterstock, page 4 George Ostertag, page 5 Jim Hinkley (top) and David M. Wyman (bottom)

Printed in China